SHARING WAYS
AND WISDOMS

SHARING WAYS AND WISDOMS

**Experiences, stories and reflections
from many cultures and countries**

BARBARA BUTLER

First published in 2001 by
KEVIN MAYHEW LTD
Buxhall, Stowmarket, Suffolk IP14 3BW
Email: info@kevinmayhewltd.com

9 8 7 6 5 4 3 2 1 0

ISBN 1 84003 708 3
Catalogue No 1500416

Cover illustration taken from a painting by Petra Rohr Rouendaal
Cover design by Jonathan Stroulger
Edited by Katherine Laidler
Typesetting by Louise Selfe
Printed and bound in Great Britain

Contents

Foreword

It is quite often said these days that the different Christian communities across the world are becoming more and more irreconcilably diverse – in style of worship, ethics, organisation, theological idiom and so on. What's sad about this is the underlying assumption that diversity is *bound* to be irreconcilable, that different ways of being Christian are always a mutual threat. But the only way of showing that this is not necessarily so is to look and listen carefully and patiently. And the paradox is that it is in this process that you discover not just 'reconciled diversity', to use an overworked churchy cliché, but the kind of unity that matters and that will survive: the unity that comes from *recognition*.

Recognition is the act of discovering that a bridge for understanding has been made before ever you have tried to start building. That is why, in this context, recognition within the worldwide Christian community is an experience of grace. Read a passage like Rafael Amor's 'Do Not Call Me "Stranger"' in this book (page 47), and you can see what this grace of recognition entails, what it challenges and overthrows. The texts in this book are drawn from as wide a variety of cultural and political settings as you could imagine; but any reader will, I believe, sense the spark of recognisability that carries from one story to the next. By the time you have finished reading (for the first time; these are stories that will bear many readings), you may begin to see the sense in which the experience of the Christian community is fundamentally one after all. But you can only know it in and through the detail.

There will be much here that is new to many readers, even those who are fairly familiar with the 'world church'; I think especially of the material about Coptic Christians and about Rodrigues Island or Sri Lanka. We are taken beyond the headlines and beyond the stereotypes and invited to something of the free and generous responses that these stories and reflections themselves witness to. Those who have had the privilege of being involved with Christians Aware, the charity which Barbara Butler has led with such vision and commitment for a decade or more, will recognise the 'house style' of this organisation – the conversation and sharing that consistently refuse to align just with party or interest groups but enable precisely that growth in *wisdom* that the aims of Christians Aware presuppose. We owe a great debt to Barbara for bringing together the conversational symphony of this book: a major sign of hope for the unity that really matters in the Church – and the world – the shared reality of love, prayer, forgiveness and renewal in Jesus.

ROWAN WILLIAMS
Archbishop of Wales

INTRODUCTION

Sharing Ways and Wisdoms

This book includes accounts of and by Christians and others in many countries around the world. They are people from many cultures and many situations, including those of poverty and persecution, conflict and struggle. They are people and communities of faith and dignity, courage and hope. The stories are both factual and fictional, and they are offered to the reader or listener – for the stories may be told or read aloud – as a way into other worlds and other wisdoms. The suggestions for reflection, discussion and action may perhaps enable readers to see more clearly the contrasts and comparisons with their own situations.

The hope of this book is that the 'sharing of ways and wisdoms' will be an experience which may change those who read it or listen to it, as any of us may have changed if we had travelled around the world or lived through some of the events. I hope that the stories and encounters offered, mainly through my work with Christians Aware, will give an insight into other people's stories, their visions and cultures, their ways of living and working, their joys and sorrows, their faiths, their wisdoms. I hope that our faith will be in the people and in their wisdom in living through the culture or faith which has given them the vision without which all people perish.

The faith of this book is that every person's vision, culture and pilgrimage will be taken seriously. I hope that more of us may come to understand, trust and respect the people we encounter and thus respect their ways of life, and also empathise when ways have been lost through war, oppression and poverty.

In Christians Aware, an educational and international charity, we offer a variety of opportunities for listening, encounter, learning and reflection, so that understanding and trust may grow between people of many countries and cultures and between Christians and people of other faiths. The hope is that people may work together to overcome injustice.

I took a group of Christians from Britain and Kenya to visit a Tanzanian Christian community near to the coast, where the people are both Muslim and Christian. The visitors asked their Tanzanian host how he managed to live with Muslims and whether he had converted any of them. The host explained that in his part of Africa Muslims and Christians had lived side by side since the seventh century CE. He had been brought up with Muslims, and knew them as serious people, people he could talk to about the issues facing the country, people he could work with on development issues. He shared his Christian faith with the Muslims, and also listened to them talking about their faith.

The contributions of individual people, however small the contributions and however shy or unknown the people, may add up to something which may influence not only individuals who listen but nations and the world. The climate of opinion in a country emerges from the spreading out of the attitudes and opinions of the ordinary people.

An African Christian evangelist has a ministry of washing and caring for the feet of those who have walked for many hundreds of miles in search of food and water, to visit the poor and ill, to school and later to work, perhaps in fields and forests. The evangelist is meeting the most urgent needs of his people, regardless of the trouble to himself. He is always tired but he is giving those he serves a new life with their renewed feet, feet they depend upon. People may not have walked for hundreds of miles and they may not have sores, blisters and bugs which can be seen, but many have made very difficult journeys and have terrible scars which need love and attention. The scars may never be known and therefore never healed unless there is friendship and trust.

An Indian friend committed his life to homeless and suffering people even into his old age partly because he had experienced suffering and division at first hand. He was living in the Punjab in 1947 during its division into India and Pakistan and witnessed the carnage as the people panicked in their attempts to rush to safe areas. Thousands of people were slaughtered and thousands more were displaced. Terence Khushal turned his college into a refugee centre where he never spared himself in providing physical and spiritual support to desperate people, often at great personal risk. He later worked in Nigeria during the civil war and when he was over 80 years old he went back to India to work with Tibetan refugees. Terence dedicated his life to his work to build up understanding and respect between people of different faiths and cultures whilst himself living in a single room.

There is a strand of Christianity which has always linked God and the ordinary life of the people in a healthy and holistic approach. There need be no separation, for God may be known in all things and in all people, no matter how hidden he may seem to be. Many of the early Celtic crosses have scenes from the Bible on one side, and scenes from everyday life on the other side. Salvadorian crosses also depict everyday life and concerns at the heart of Christianity. The early Celtic Christians prayed to God at every time of the day and even at night, and they did not separate prayer from their other activities, but prayed and sang on every occasion. Nothing was secular. The people prayed with the understanding that the Christ and Mary were joining in with the work, the cooking, farming, and with life in general. The early Celtic Christians had a lot in common with many African Christians who are people of community, poor and yet generous in their welcome of the stranger, hardworking and humorous, struggling for a future. A group of Kenyans who visited Britain tried to sum up their people and finally, after much discussion, said that they are 'people in pain who still dance'.

The most powerful example of a holistic approach to life and faith I have experienced today is in some of the African churches, where services are long, perhaps four or five hours, and sometimes the services carry on overnight, because there is no separation between worship of God and God in all things. Nothing is secular. A group in Mozambique went to a Christian youth festival which included singing, dancing and praying. There were also sermons and meditations, and it all lasted for about 21 hours.

There is a legend of a holy man who lived long ago in a remote village in India. He lived alone, growing his food in his small garden and he spent his time making beautiful images which expressed his vision of the Divine. He spent several months making each image. He began in contemplation and then he carved the image in soft beeswax, taking time and great care over each section. He then mixed clay and pasted it all over the image and allowed it to dry in the bright sun. He warmed the beeswax, and poured it out of the clay, and then he came to the most wonderful stage in his work. He chose a suitable metal for the image, bronze or silver or gold. He melted the metal and poured it into the clay mould, allowing it to set. Finally he cracked the clay mould to reveal the image, bright and shining, one of his visions of the Divine. He kept the image in his small home until he found the right person to give it to, someone who would appreciate it. He then went on to make another image.

The reputation of the holy man spread for many hundreds of miles. The king of a distant realm heard about him, and sent one of his servants in search of a beautiful image. The servant walked for many months and finally found the village, the simple home and the holy man. He explained that his master, the king of a large kingdom, would like one of the images. The holy man asked questions about the king, trying to get to know him a little. The servant was impatient. Suddenly he took out a bag of coins, the money the king had given him to buy the image. The holy man was very upset, and explained that he never took money for his work, but simply wanted it to go to people who would appreciate it and who would benefit from it. The servant was perplexed and, momentarily, undecided about what to do next. Then he decided. He threw the bag of money on to the floor, grabbed the beautiful image, and ran.

When the king's servant had gone, the holy man was at first dazed and then ill for a long time. He tried to make a new image but could not manage to create anything which expressed his vision. He made image after image, and had to melt them all down because they were very dull. Finally he closed his home and set off on the journey to find the king. He walked for a long time and at last found the king's palace. He waited outside the palace doors for several weeks and eventually the king gave orders for him to be let in. He entered the great hall and saw the king at the far end. He explained what had happened to his image, that he never accepted money for his work and that the king's servant, following the wishes of the king, had given the money which had been a rejection of everything he stood for, a rejection of him, which had made it impossible for him to work creatively again. 'A mistake was made,' he said. The king thought for several minutes surrounded by the heavy silence and then he said, 'Yes, a mistake was made.' The bag of money was returned to the king and the holy man was free to go home, his gift restored. The first image he made was a present for the king.

The unthinking action of the king had oppressed and disabled the holy man. The king and his servant had assumed that the holy man would have the same values as themselves. They had assumed that because they wanted his gifts they could buy them. It was only when the king took the time to listen to the holy man that he realised that someone different from himself was in front of him, someone he could perhaps never fully understand, but someone he could respect. The holy man also came to understand the king because he took the trouble to make the long journey to meet him. How often, in every society, are people disabled because others do not have time to notice or appreciate their gifts or their most pressing needs?

I hope this book may offer a link between the readers and

the people and stories in it. If we allow the people behind the stories to become real to us, and even to change us, we may ourselves become peacemakers in the most dynamic sense. We will no longer wish to see other people, in other areas, cultures, faiths, or countries, as separate and different. We will see the other person or people as real, as visionary, creative, destructive, suffering, ordinary and God-filled. As this book hopes to offer a bridge towards understanding and trust, so the readers may offer many bridges of understanding towards others. But, like the Indian holy man in the legend, we all need to make the effort to move, to make the journey.

Barbara Butler

Bridge

Svenua Savie

When the word *bridge* is heard, we immediately picture two sides that are connected. The main idea in the meaning of this word is joining together. It takes a lot of time and strength to build a bridge, because we need to get from one side to another; and yet it takes only a few seconds to destroy it, because the joint is fragile. Years and years had passed before the bridge across the Danube connecting Petrovaradin and Novi Sad was built; only one well-targeted bomb was enough to destroy it for ever. A lot of energy was needed to unite two worlds by this bridge: the Orthodox world living on one side and the Catholic world living on the other – a single bomb managed to divide them.

Bridges are constructions that we are proud of, but, at the same time, they are constructions of the spirit, which join people and objects. This is why the bridge in Novi Sad was not just a physical construction; it was a construction of emotions since every citizen had somebody or something in the other part of town. The pupils of the high school in Sremski Karlovci used to cross this bridge every day on their way to school. They were going to the other side to gain knowledge, find their first love and spend hours and days that were to remain a part of their youthful memories. But the bridge is destroyed, and it is no longer possible for the citizens of Novi Sad to visit the three beautiful Catholic churches of Petrovaradin every day as they did in the past. Those who had their peaceful oases in the Fruska Gora Mountain cannot find their rest there any more. We, from here, cannot go to them who are over there, and it hurts!

The bombardment of the bridge in Novi Sad symbolises the division between nations, parts of the world, the division within ourselves. The bombardment of the bridge in Novi

The Great Bridge of Hope
Solomon Raj

Sad is only one of a series of bombardments in our (former) country – including the beautiful bridge in Mostar. . . . Bridges are disappearing, the bridges that join us and remind us of the fact that it *is* possible to live together.

And today, as we stand in front of our destroyed bridge, each of us recalls how we lived with it, and we all cry. Destroying the bridge in Novi Sad as a strategic point has moved the emotional point of our balance and now we are limping in search of support.

A Storyteller

Beullah Candappa is a storyteller. Her stories are mostly folk tales, legends, poems and songs from Asia and around the world. They reflect the atmosphere, character and culture of the places they are set in. One of her stories is set in the Philippines, where a tiny but strong and quick-witted girl, who lived with her parents, was captured by the god of the gulf. She refused all temptations to wealth and comfort, and managed to return to her parents.

Beullah is someone who comes into a room for the first time, to meet a group of people she has never met before, and immediately creates an atmosphere of friendship and inspiration. I well remember her joining a large group of Kenyan visitors on a camp in Yorkshire. She brought along drums, gongs, artefacts and her stories, which she told long into the night, sitting on the floor and surrounded by mesmerised listeners. Her own real life story is as fascinating as any fable. Once at a conference gathering she held eighty people spellbound when she told them of the time she spent in Calcutta during the Second World War, a time she refers to in her story, a time of suffering but also of making new friends, one of whom was her Jesuit teacher. She returned to India, and to Calcutta, in 1997 and requested a visit to the school she had attended as a refugee in wartime. She met many pupils and teachers but was completely bowled over when she met her old teacher, now in his nineties. She is a powerful and enchanting storyteller.

My Vision

Beullah Candappa

I was born in Burma, the eldest girl in a family of ten children. When the Japanese occupied Burma in 1942, we suddenly became refugees for four years. Thank God, we were taken into schools run by Catholic missionaries in India, and when the war was over we returned to Burma.

Burma was (and still is) in a very troubled state, so eventually my family came to England. I married a Sri Lankan, Leslie Candappa, an architect and abstract painter. When my children were growing up, I trained as a mature student to be a teacher in London. I taught in a primary school for fourteen years but I have now given up teaching to be a full-time, freelance storyteller.

I have been telling stories for about 24 years, travelling and telling stories from all over the world (folk tales, myths, legends, stories for religious education, nursery rhymes, poems, riddles, songs, hymns). I have also run workshops on the art of storytelling, workshops for RE teachers, for the under-fives, for the physically and mentally disabled, for 'evergreens' (senior citizens), and for radio and television.

Why tell stories? Here are some reasons.

With ten children in our family, my father was a wonderful storyteller. He could spin 'fairy gold'. A spider's web became a magic carpet which transported us everywhere. We could even reach the rainbow . . . some day.

So, inspired by my father, I feel as if I'm on a pilgrimage; travelling the road, moved by the sense of religion – the numinous – hoping to open this special door to all who listen, to the sense of the spiritual, the mystical . . . to a sense of wonder, beauty, reverence, awe and mystery.

Through telling stories I am trying to give children the opportunity to learn to listen, to exercise that rare power of mental visualisation, emphasising the strong links between listening to a story and children learning to read. And, through storytelling, I am trying to build bridges of understanding between cultures, religions, nations; to help all listeners to reach for the stars and beyond.

Reflection

'I'm on a pilgrimage . . . hoping to open this special door to all who listen . . . to the sense of the spiritual, the mystical . . .'

Discussion and Action

Beullah's father could spin 'fairy gold'. Share some of the 'fairy gold' you would put into your own stories, whether they are fables, folk tales and legends, or the real-life stories of yourself or someone close to you.

The Tale of Two Sisters

An Adventure of Faith from the Early Twentieth Century

In the year 1903, twin girls were born in a small house in Handsworth, Birmingham. The babies were very small and weak. The following year they were taken to Great Ormond Street Hospital for treatment, and started to walk only at the age of three.

This shaky start did not prevent the two girls from growing up healthy. Both wanted to train as nurses, but in those days twins were not allowed to start their training together, so Isabel started first and Elsie later. The year was 1924.

Soon the girls decided that Africa was the place for them and in 1930 they prepared for this great adventure with the Universities Mission to Central Africa. They took courses in dispensary, theatre work, anaesthetics, dentistry, and they also learnt Swahili. They also spent three months at the Convent of the Community of the Sacred Passion in Duxhurst, Surrey, where the Sisters gave them instructions on the type of food they would eat and the life they would lead. Here, they also learnt to use paraffin hurricane lamps and paraffin stoves.

These are short sections from their diary:

We arrive: We sailed from Tilbury, on the *Llanstephen Castle*, on 17 March 1931. The journey lasted for seven weeks and we were met at Zanzibar by Archdeacon Woodward who had come out in a small boat to meet us. Then followed a happy two weeks spent at the Mission Hospital near the Cathedral, in Zanzibar.

Two weeks later, we boarded a small Indian boat which took us to our destination on the mainland. We were the only white people on that boat. The other people were all Indians, and the journey lasted for two weeks. On arrival at Lindi, we found a letter saying that, early the next morning, a lorry would come to take us to Masasi. We spent that night in a little mud hut, and we were brought bread and tea, and a small fish in oil.

Sure enough, a lorry arrived at 4 am the next day. It was loaded with mission stores and our luggage, and in this transport we bumped along for 200 miles. It was dark when we reached the Mission Station. People came out to meet us with hurricane lamps. After an evening meal, we were taken to our little mud houses, about 50 yards apart, and each with a hole in the wall for a window.

We were so excited, but we couldn't write home immediately, as we had intended. There were insects and lizards all over the tables! So, instead, we retired to bed under the mosquito nets. What joy! We really had arrived in Africa!

Missionary life: As missionaries, we were poor but happy. Our allowance was 20 pounds a year and we were thought rich by the Africans, which we truly were as we did not have anything to worry about. There was very little money in circulation because nearly everything was transacted by barter – a reel of cotton and a needle, for 100 eggs, etc.

Food was a problem if we ran short. We lived out of tins, and, if lucky, we could get 100 eggs for a shilling (5p), hens as big as pigeons for 6*d* (2.5p), rice 100lb for a shilling (5p).

Incident at Liuli: The mission houses at Liuli were on a hill, a little way from the lake, while the hospital was on the shore. One night, I (Isabel) was called out because a woman, who was said to be dead, had been brought in from the hills. When I got to the shore, I found about two hundred people wailing and the 'dead' woman being carried in a machila. I examined her and she did not move, but her pulse was quite good. I then asked the dispensary boy to get a teaspoonful of ammoniated tincture of quinine, which I gave her. She sat up immediately. Oh, how everyone screamed! I kept the woman in hospital because I found that the trouble was, she had been supposed to die, as her spirit was said to have caused a drought. She stayed in hospital until it rained and then all went well.

During my time at Liuli, there was much work to do among leprosy patients at the two camps, two miles, and eight miles away on the lake shore. We visited the camps twice a week to give injections and general nursing care. There were 450 patients.

One of the many exciting things that happened there was a visit from Dr Muir, then the greatest living specialist on leprosy. He came to examine all the patients and to advise us on how to care for them. He found we had 88 people who had been cured, or whose leprosy was 'burnt out', and he said they could be sent to their homes.

We had a thanksgiving service and all the cured patients came into the mission church. It was a most exciting service, with everyone joining in. After the service, most were crying because they wanted to stay in the colony. Some had been having treatment for more than 20 years and, for them, the camp was home. We allowed them to stay and help if they wished.

The War: By August 1939 news of the impending war reached us. At the end of August 1940 Elsie returned to England to get married to Joseph Neave, who had done wonderful work in Africa, building and repairing churches. In January 1941 I left Nyasaland for Capetown in South Africa to try my luck at getting a passage to England. I went by lorry to Blantyre, then on by lorry to Salisbury (Harare), Southern Rhodesia (Zimbabwe). On the way, we had to stop at Tete to cross the Zambesi on a hand-propelled ferry. From there, I caught the train for a two-and-a-half-day journey to Capetown.

On arriving at Capetown, I went to the Union Castle office but they told me that it might be three weeks before a boat was able to leave for England. I did not know what I would do, or where I would stay. I eventually remembered Mrs Stephenson, one of 150 visitors to Nyasaland, whom I had talked to one evening at Liuli. As the coaches were leaving, she had slipped an envelope into my hand, with 5 pounds for the leprosy patients and also her address in Capetown.

After trying a few Stephensons listed in the telephone directory, at last I got my Mrs Stephenson. What a joy! I was with her for three weeks. We went to the Union Castle offices every morning, and one day I was told, 'Your boat, the *Arundel Castle*, leaves at 11 am.' I was sent off with winter and summer clothes, a blanket and a tin of biscuits. There were only 40 passengers.

We started off in a convoy, but after four days woke up to find that we were quite alone. When we got to the west coast, we heard that the British battleship *Hood* had been sunk and that we were to return to Capetown. Our boat dropped depth charges at regular intervals.

We had been on the return journey for two days when the German battleship *Bismarck* was reported sunk. Then we were allowed to resume our journey to England. We rescued about 300 distressed sailors on our way. We took on some 600 Iraqi refugees when we stopped outside Gibraltar. The refugees came out in small boats and had to climb up the side of the liner. We helped them over the side. As I was pulling some over, I said to the man who was standing beside me, 'Can you help?' He did, and, to my surprise, I found out later that he was Governor of Gibraltar.

Reflection 1

What courage it must have taken to make a journey into the unknown, to meet new people, to share with them and to live in new ways.

Discussion and Action

1. The two missionaries were 'poor but happy'. How far does money determine happiness in our communities/country? What changes might we make in our lifestyles, which would reduce our spending of money and at the same time increase our happiness?

2. Isabel's journey home was fraught with danger. She and some of her fellow travellers were able to help refugees. Are there ways in which we can help refugees who come to our country from situations of danger?
   Find out who are the refugees who live near to you, get to know them, listen to their stories, and work with them.

Reflection 2

He sent them out to preach the kingdom of God and to heal the sick, after saying to them, 'Take nothing with you for the journey: no stick, no beggar's bag, no food, no money, not even an extra shirt.' *Luke 9:2-3*

Jesus Sends out the Twelve Disciples
Francis Hoyland

HURT AND HOPE –
DISPLACED PEOPLE
AND REFUGEES

Introduction

Meeting refugees brings home the sad fact that they are ordinary people facing extraordinary circumstances. More ordinary people in the world today are facing upheaval than ever before. Hardly a week goes by without news coverage of people who are refugees somewhere in the world. The problem is that media coverage of refugee peoples is erratic and there are many sad situations that are never known by the world outside them.

There are also internal refugees, people who are displaced in their own countries. They are often overlooked altogether and their plight may be terrible.

As the suffering situations in the world grow, it seems that the patience, will and resources of those who are not suffering grow less. Perhaps it has always been difficult for most people to welcome the stranger. Elie Wiesel wrote of refugees, 'You might even say that they come out of nowhere to usurp someone else's place. Foreigners are shrouded in mystery. . . . They plunge into a world that was there before they were and which has no need of them. They arouse fear, just as they themselves fear.'

The opportunities for refugees to find a new home and to build a new life are not very great at the beginning of the twenty-first century, even though the 1948 Universal Declaration of Human Rights recognised the right of every person to seek asylum from persecution in another country. America no longer asks for 'your tired, your poor, your huddled masses yearning to breathe free' (as written on the Statue of Liberty). Europe is in danger perhaps of becoming 'fortress Europe', focusing on its own problems, which are many. Much time and energy are taken up in deciding who are genuine refugees, which is necessary perhaps, but very difficult. The procedures for dealing with asylum seekers vary from country to country in Europe. There is a very complicated process in the UK now. Most refugees, in fact, are given homes in the Developing World.

The sufferings of most refugees are great and their need for patience, understanding and care is equally great. Most refugees wish to talk about their experiences, and sometimes to write them down, to help them in coming to terms with what has happened. Loneliness, homesickness, vulnerability and culture shock are lessened when there are opportunities to share with those who are sympathetic.

Ailsa Moore was the Director of the Ockenden Venture in the 1990s.* She has also been a teacher in the UK and Africa. She has written regularly on former Yugoslavia, and especially on the human side of the tragedy for people who have had more than enough of fleeing, who are divided, often homeless and normally ill. On one occasion she met a group of refugees who were living under a cluster of trees in Split. A more comfortable place had been offered in a centre, but it was rejected because the home under the trees was more accessible for women whose husbands might be looking for them. A move to a centre would simply add them to the lists of the unknown and insecure.

Ailsa was always impressed during her travels by the way so many people cared about the children of the war. People in Vukovar spoke to her about the orphans: 'Maybe we can succeed in preventing them from becoming embittered losers, but rather young people who have had a homeland which they loved and which they want to rebuild.'

On one occasion Ailsa visited a tented refugee camp of over 1,000 people beside the sea in Split. She gave gifts of clothes to two little girls and, in the middle of the camp, was beautifully entertained by the mother. Many people wanted to talk and to tell their stories.

* The Ockenden Venture is a charity, founded in 1951, which offers training, healthcare and education for refugees around the world, including Tibetan people in India, Afghans in Pakistan, refugees from the Sudan, and those arriving in the UK from many countries, including Eastern Europe.

In another camp Ailsa met people who had gone there having lived all their lives in good homes but who were now forced to live in very different and very difficult circumstances, and nevertheless had smiles of welcome. Their houses had been blown up and their land mined and yet they offered coffee – the whole month's supply.

One day Ailsa went to a place where there had been shelling and where the tops of the houses had been blown off. They visited displaced people who had taken shelter in a badly damaged primary school. One of those they met was a remarkable man in a recently acquired wheelchair who chased madly around the place, making everyone laugh.

Ailsa travels regularly to Croatia and Bosnia. She has said that 'Every minute of a visit is filled with experiences that tear into you.' Her writing of suffering and hope is both moving and encouraging.

Every Little Counts

Ailsa Moore

In 1993 I was sitting in my office at the Ockenden Venture in Woking when the phone rang. It was a call from the Bosnian Embassy in Zagreb, Croatia. A lady speaking in clear English asked if I could please help refugees from Bosnia. They were desperate. They had people with cancer needing urgent help. I felt very moved by the emotion in the speaker's voice. I asked if I could be sent the medical details, but could make no promises.

The papers arrived by fax. I sent them to the Royal Marsden Hospital in London. Could they help? Quickly the reply came. They had selected one person, suffering from lymphoma, that they felt they could treat. I knew that this did not mean that the problem was solved. I still needed a visa and air ticket but I felt confident that these hurdles would be overcome.

I rang the Bosnian Embassy in Croatia and the same lady came on the phone. I told her the good news that the Marsden would accept one of the group. I could hear this being translated. Then there was spontaneous cheering. I explained how sorry I was not to be able to help them all. 'You are helping one, you are helping all!' came the excited reply.

A year later, I visited that same embassy. There I was told that this act of helping one out of many meant so much. It meant that somebody had listened and cared, and because of that everyone gained courage. I will always remember this.

Nothing is ever too little. The lady we brought over here is still here, and still receiving treatment. We love her dearly, not just for herself but for what she meant to others, perhaps not so fortunate.

Reflection

I plead with you to be merciful.
With you who have the face of a demon
and command thorns and nails
and with you who have poured night into our shoes
and make no distinction between good
and infamous or unreasonable news.
With you who have enveloped towns in darkness
and tempted ploughland into infertility,
who have left islands bereft of their seas,
and the sea of its ships,
and anchorages of their shelter,
dressed us in Lenten clothes,
forced us underground
and forbidden the holy import of words.
Jaksa Fiamengo

Discussion and Action

'You are helping one, you are helping all.' What does this statement tell us of the community amongst the Bosnian people? What are our communities of hope? How may we be challenged in them?

A Story of Courage

Ailsa Moore

In 1994 my organisation, the Ockenden Venture, was running a project in Krajina, a Serb-occupied part of Croatia. We were helping to provide basic accommodation for displaced Serbian people and, where we could, to bring some comfort and relief.

My field officer came across a family with a child who had cystic fibrosis. The child's name was Anamarija. She was 4 years old and dependent on drugs to ease her condition. In Krajina, during the war, there were no drugs. Geoff set about finding some means of helping this little child.

He found a supply of suitable drugs and managed to get them to the family. Imagine the happiness this brought. The child's suffering would be lessened, at least for a time.

This wonderful feeling was best described by the child herself. She drew a picture. On the left she drew her face as she felt on Sunday – dark, sad and without hope. On Monday when the drugs arrived, she shows her delight by drawing her happy, smiling face on the right. How well this young child of 4 expresses her feeling of courage and hope. We called the picture 'Sunday-Monday'.

Reflection 1

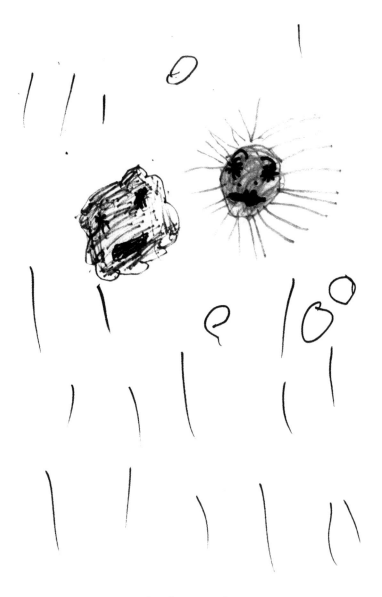

Sunday-Monday

Discussion and Action

Draw your own 'Sunday-Monday' picture and explain it to others. Where may we offer a change from Sunday to Monday?

Reflection 2

In the Tibetan philosophy of 'Satyagraha' people must be rigorously trained to seek the truth and to insist upon non-violent action. This means removing from the mind and spirit all need for vengeance, all feelings of hate and greed. It requires the cultivation of compassion and love and the showing of uncompromising insistence on the pursuit of these principles. We must look therefore to ourselves, and realise that we are often the abusers, lacking patience and being concerned more with our own image than with the welfare of others.

Discussion and Action

How may we begin to free ourselves from the negative qualities which stand in the way of compassion and love?

Should we work for spiritual freedom before we can seek human rights for all, or should we work for human rights so that people may achieve spiritual freedom?

Refugees from Burma

Inside Burma the military government, with its large army, is an oppressive dictatorship which continually suppresses the movement towards democracy. The National League for Democracy, led by Aung San Sui Kyi, won a landslide victory in the 1990 elections but its members are threatened and detained. Many of them are refugees. An estimated 120,000 Burmese people are in refugee camps, mostly in Thailand. The people are trying to organise themselves in the camps, to cater for the needs of the children and to become a community. A letter from a camp in Northern Thailand reads:

> We come from Karenni State. . . . We are living in a refugee camp in Northern Thailand. We have been here for three years. There are about 3,000 refugees living in our camp and there are about 10,000 refugees living in three other camps. We live in bamboo houses, we grow vegetables and fruit. We also have chickens, pigs, turkeys and ducks, and we eat rice every day. Some refugees go to the jungle every day to find food. We have a nursery school, a primary school and a middle school. We play volleyball and football. We also like to sing and play guitar. When we finish Eighth Standard we can go on to high school in Camp 5.
>
> We are refugees because Burmese soldiers are fighting in Karenni State and we cannot go home. We are fighting for independence from the Burmese military government. Many Karenni people still live in Karenni State and it is very dangerous. We hope one day we will return home.

The Chin people live in the north-west of Burma, which borders on to a turbulent area of India. There are about 800,000 Chin people living in Burma, and 90 per cent of them are Christian. The Chin Christians have recently celebrated the

Flight into Egypt
Francis Hoyland

centenary of Christianity in their land. They put up a cross on a hill, but were ordered to take it down by the military authorities. When they refused, the army arrested 26 Chin pastors and burnt down the churches. The Chin Christians have to do forced labour on Sundays. David Yam is someone who went to a Buddhist monastery for his early education and is now a Christian priest. He had to flee from Burma because he was a member of the pro-democracy movement.

Reflection

An angel of the Lord appeared in a dream to Joseph and said, 'Herod will be looking for the child in order to kill him. So get up, take the child and his mother and escape to Egypt, and stay there until I tell you to leave.' Joseph got up, took the child and his mother, and left during the night for Egypt, where he stayed until Herod died. *Matthew 2:13-14*

Refugees from Iraq

People flee from Iraq because they have been persecuted or because they fear that they will be persecuted. Some go over into Jordan, as they have since the Gulf War. Others are smuggled out across the northern border of the country. One Iraqi Christian who was smuggled out had been in prison and his father had been killed. He was able to enter Turkey with a false passport and to move from there to the UK.

Ahmed was born in 1967, into a family of four brothers and three sisters. His father and mother were Kurdish. His older brother was with the Kurdish National Democratic Front. After the end of the Iran/Iraq War in August 1988, the Iraqi army moved to the north of Iraq and started to fight the Kurds. Chemical weapons were used in many villages, and many hundreds of people were killed. Ahmed's brother fled. At this stage Ahmed was a student. He was arrested and then released after ten days. The teacher was arrested when three security men came into the classroom and tried to arrest all the students. One fled to another college, and brought other students to fight. One student took a pistol and shot a security guard. Ahmed then ran away and left for Iran with other Kurds, travelling on foot through the mountains.

One refugee came from a professional family; both his parents were dentists. He completed high school and then preferred art to medicine. He was taken from his university, blindfolded, when he refused to join the Iraqi Baath party. He was given electric shock treatment and released in the desert. He was fortunate to be found, and his uncle, who lived in Kuwait and had American nationality, supported him to continue his studies in Kuwait.

After the invasion of Kuwait by Iraq in 1990, which began the Gulf War, pressure was put on the student to join the Iraqi army, but he refused. He had to stay in hiding and keep moving from house to house. Finally his mother received a message that he was accused of being a traitor, because he was buying and selling weapons to Iraq's enemies. This was a false accusation but he knew that he had to leave. He joined a cattle truck, dressed as an Egyptian, and was very fortunate to enter Jordan when his passport was stamped carelessly, in the middle of the night. Once in Jordan he was accepted as a refugee by the United Nations High Commission for Refugees. After two days he travelled to Cyprus, where he stayed as a cleaner and swineherd. Cyprus refused to allow him to stay permanently and he returned to Jordan where he enlisted the help of the United Nations and eventually found work.

Life in Iraq is not only one of fear of oppression but a terrible physical struggle for most people, and especially for those with children. The children, as ordinary and necessary foods are no longer available to them, are increasingly mal-nourished and therefore vulnerable to disease. The infant mortality rate is growing. The hospitals are struggling with impossible shortages of everything from drugs to bed sheets.

> Dear Jesus, strengthen my faith and hope
>   and put love in my heart.
> Garnish my soul with humility and patience.
> Give me wisdom and knowledge.
> Dear Jesus, fill me with your love
> and give love to my neighbour.
> *A prayer of the Syrian Orthodox Church from Mazin Farjo*

Reflection

People should never apologise for being refugees, nor should they ever despair or allow bitterness to hinder them. Refugees are often, through their pain, very strong people, and all have something to offer. The great need for refugees is that they should organise themselves, so that they have a framework to their lives and a goal. People who are not refugees may help them to do this.

Bassi Mirzania, who is herself a refugee from Iran

For many people, differences of background and experience suggest problems. Some people would go so far as to think that those who are different are dangerous, including those who are refugees.

People may especially fear those who have been tortured in their own countries. An asylum-seeker from Zaire was typical of many in that he had been seized and tortured in his own country because he was a member of the opposition to the government and had taken part in a demonstration. He managed to escape from prison and arrived in the UK where he spent six months in prison because he was travelling on false documents. He said, 'I thought I had reached safety. . . . My situation was made worse because I could not speak English very well.' Eventually a refugee community organisation arranged legal help and found him accommodation when he was released from prison.

Problems for refugees include the stress they face in being so far away from their homes and often from their families. Like the man from Zaire, they often can't speak the language of the country they are in, they have no money and no way of earning through work. Most of all, they lack people to listen to their stories.

Discussion and Action

1. How may we work to overcome prejudice against refugees and asylum-seekers in our communities?

2. Meet asylum-seekers, listen to their stories and choose one way of working with them.

Do Not Call Me 'Stranger'

Rafael Amor, from Zaire

Do not call me 'stranger' because in a mother's love we all receive the same light; in their songs, their kisses, close to their breast, they all dream about us being equal.

Do not call me 'stranger'. Do not think of where I came from. Better to think of our common destiny, and to look at where time is leading us.

Do not call me 'stranger' because your bread and your fire assuage my hunger and cold, and because your roof shelters me.

Do not call me 'stranger'. Your wheat is like mine and your hand like my own! And hunger, never overcome, wanders about everywhere, constantly changing its victims.

And you call me 'stranger' because your way drew me and because I was born in another country; because I have known other seas and sailed from other ports. And, for all that, the handkerchiefs that wave to tell us goodbye are all the same, and the same also the eyes moistened by the tears of those we leave behind. The same are the prayers and the love of those who dream of our return.

Do not call me 'stranger'. We all cry with the same voice and share the same fatigue which we carry about since the beginning of time when frontiers had not been invented, well before the arrival of those who divide and kill, of those who sell our dreams and would, one day, invent the word 'stranger'.

Do not call me 'stranger'. It is a sad word, a cold word, evocative of exile.

Do not call me 'stranger'. Watch your son run with mine, hand in hand, until the end of the road.

Do not call me 'stranger' because they understand nothing about language, about frontiers, about flags. See them go up to the heavens: a single dove carries them, united in a single flight.

Do not call me 'stranger'. Look at me straight in the eye, beyond hatred, egotism, and fear and you will see . . . I cannot be a stranger.

CARIBBEAN CALYPSO

The Tradition of the Calypso

The tradition of the calypso in the Caribbean has sprung directly out of slavery. It is the tradition of the singing of the concerns of the people, allowed in the days of slavery because it was seen as light-hearted entertainment. The slaves on the plantations were free to express themselves in song, about their lives, society, politics and religion. The calypso continues, into the twenty-first century, to offer the same colourful and creative opportunity to raise serious issues in a light, humorous and entertaining way. When I visited Barbados I heard songs on relationships, on family life and its problems, on drug problems and on AIDS. I learnt so much in one long evening spent in the calypso tent at the 'Crop-over' festival – the time when the sugar harvest ended in the past – that it provided enough material for study and discussion for several visits.

My first thought in being so warmly welcomed by friends in Barbados, with the opportunity to visit homes and to meet people all over the island, was that it is fairly amazing that the Caribbean people are willing to be so friendly with people from Europe after their shared history. The great interest many of the young people also have in Africa and in their African roots was much more to be expected.

European domination and settlement were established in the Caribbean area by force, following the journeys of exploration of Christopher Columbus at the end of the fifteenth century. The horrors of the transatlantic slave trade accompanied the development of the sugar industry and brought the people from Africa to the Caribbean, for the benefit of Europe.

Some have argued that the modern hotel has now replaced the sugar plantation as the centre of attention for European people in the Caribbean and as the place where most of the local people work.

The twentieth-century movement which brought the people

from the Caribbean to Europe was also for the benefit of Europe. In the 1940s, 50s and early 60s people in the Caribbean were recruited for work in the UK. Gary Younge in his book *No Place Like Home* tells of how his mother, who was born in Barbados, went to live in Stevenage, where he was brought up. The British Government needed people to work and put posters up all over the island asking people to go to Britain. They gave orientation classes in which people were advised to wear woolly hats and flannelette pyjamas in the cold climate. His mother's fare was paid to England, where she became a nurse and then a teacher. She brought up her family in an atmosphere which mostly veered between curiosity and cold hostility. She needed more than a woolly hat to survive. There was also some friendship which made it all possible. She was typical of many.

Even now, at the beginning of the twenty-first century, attitudes to Caribbean people in the UK are not always friendly. A Bajan, as the people of Barbados are called, who welcomed me to his home and Christian community in the capital city, Bridgetown, came to England to visit friends. He witnessed a robbery in a pub in Yorkshire and reported this to the police, only to find, to his astonishment, that he was the first suspect. The fact that he is a magistrate in Barbados made no difference at all to those who were so suspicious of him.

Over the last forty years people have also come from Africa and Asia to the UK and a multi-racial, inter-faith and multi-cultural society has been developing. This has not always been easy and there is still a lot of work to be done to create a society where all people are valued and respected, and where people of all walks of life and racial origins mix freely with each other and feel at home.

Many people whose parents came from the Caribbean, where they were born, have said that they do not feel completely at home anywhere. Some of them have travelled to the home of their ancestors in Africa, and also to the countries their parents came from in the Caribbean. They have found common ground in both places but also much that is different. One person, a black writer, said that when he went to Jamaica he was stopped on the streets and told that he was British. The reason given was that he was walking too quickly. In the UK, which is his permanent home, he can't help remembering that he is a member of a minority community.

The Wailing Song

Victoria Amediku

A poor man strums on his guitar
A song the words of which I cannot understand
yet in my spirit I know
it was a wailing song.

I have heard that sound before
of anguished suppressed souls
crying out to the maker above
who already hears and knows their plight.

He has eyes and ears everywhere,
ears that hear the faintest sound an infant makes,
eyes that see even the tiniest detail of its form
while being knit in the depths of the womb.

He hears the wailing
of those being trod on by others.
He cares and his heart aches for them
for he made each one in his image.

The wailing of those driven from their homes,
denied the dignity of life,
made to feel they do not count
in a world they've been born into.

I hear the same song
from the slaves on the oceans, the plantations,
from the Aborigines down under,
from Africa, Asia and the so-called Third World.

The Stone of Weeping

The World Council of Churches held a mission conference in Salvador in Brazil in 1997. Brazil was, like most of the Caribbean islands, a place where slaves were taken and used until almost a hundred years ago. For over 300 years ship after ship brought hundreds of African people across the Atlantic to the sugar plantations. Today Brazil has a larger number of citizens of African origin than any country in Africa with the exception of Nigeria.

The World Council of Churches conference included people of every country and race and people of all ages. One morning during the conference everyone went down to the docks where the slaves who had survived the hazardous journey were unloaded from the ships. A simple service was held by the stone of weeping; the stone in the market place where families were split up as members were sold to different owners; the stone which had known much weeping over the centuries. During the service everyone confessed, white people and black people together, that people of all races had profited from the slave trade, that all were implicated. People shared their grief for the sufferings of the slaves and stated their determination to resist oppression wherever it may show itself in today's world.

Discussion and Action

1. Make a group definition of slavery. Where is there slavery in the world today and what can be done to end it?

2. How much do you know about the lives of people from the Caribbean who now live in the UK? Strive to meet people and to share the issues they face.

3. Speak out whenever you experience racist behaviour or attitudes.

Photo: Barbara Butler

Carnival Time in Barbados

PAIN AND PROMISE
IN THE MIDDLE EAST

Introduction

Palestine was the area around Jerusalem which came under British administration in 1917, after the collapse of the Turkish Empire. The Arab people already lived in the area with a small number of Jewish people. Between the First and Second World Wars many more Jewish people moved into the area, encouraged to do so by the British Government.

Following the Second World War, and the horror of the Holocaust which was the culmination of many centuries of persecution of Jewish people, more Jews went into Palestine from all over Europe and then from all over the world. At first the British Government discouraged this movement, and some Jewish people were sent away, leading to violence between the Jews and the British. The United Nations proposed the establishment of two states, one Jewish and one Arab, in 1947-8, but fighting broke out and the plan could not be put into practice peacefully. Instead there was war, at the end of which the land of Palestine was taken over by the new State of Israel. Some land was also gained by Jordan.

In 1967 the West Bank was taken from Jordan and occupied by Israel. It has formed the focus for the new Palestinian State. Many Palestinian people, however, are still living all over the world as the result of the troubles. The Jewish settlers who moved into the West Bank and other areas occupied by Israel – including the Golan Heights, taken from Syria, and Gaza, taken from Egypt – are very reluctant to leave their homes as the Palestinian State develops.

Jerusalem is the religious centre for three faiths: Christian, Jewish and Muslim. Agreement between Israel and Palestine on the future of Jerusalem remains the dream of people of the three faiths.

There are many people, Jewish, Christian and Muslim, who are working for peace and reconciliation in the Middle East today. I introduce just a few of them, including my friend, Najwa Farah.

Najwa Farah: A Palestinian Christian

It is vital for people outside the Middle East to have the opportunity to encounter the Palestinian people and culture, their struggle and longing for home. The people have had a century-long journey which has largely been one of suffering and rejection, but, remarkably, hope has never been lost. Najwa Farah has said that, 'A writer is moved to write because she experiences something. That something might seem trivial or insignificant, it might be the name of a person, a memory or a smell, an atmosphere, a remark, or a whole saga.'

It is easy to see from my brief summary of Najwa's life, which follows, that her experience has been far from trivial. She has lived totally from within the Palestinian people's pilgrimage of suffering and tragedy, a pilgrimage in search of an answer to the question, 'Who are we?' Najwa is a Palestinian Christian, and the hope she offers is the hope offered by Christ, whose cross, 'was the link between heaven and earth . . . a ladder soaring upwards'. Najwa is a link person, a link between the time of Jesus and the earliest Christians, from whom she is descended, and the wider Christian world; a link between Christians and Muslims; a link between the Middle East and the rest of the world; and a link between those who have suffered and those who have not.

Najwa Farah comes from an Arab Christian family and was born in Nazareth when it was part of Palestine under the British Mandate. Her father was a member of the Greek Orthodox Church and her mother was an Anglican. Najwa remembers her father as witty and intelligent and a lover of poetry. Her mother made the deepest impression on her. She was a well-educated and devout Christian who spent a lot of time teaching her children and shielding them from the more unpleasant aspects of life in the Middle East. Najwa grew up in a cultured and happy home where she learnt to love Arab litera-ture and poetry, and, later, to love English novels, plays and poetry. Sunday afternoons were spent by the family in visiting relatives and walking on the hills of Nazareth. She remembers a harmonious ecumenical childhood, and peaceful and friendly relations with Muslims, who were close neighbours.

When schooldays were over, Najwa was one of very few girls to be trained as a teacher in the Women's Training College in Jerusalem. She remembers her college days as difficult ones in a colonial institution where the local culture and people were not appreciated, at a time when the British Government was implementing the Balfour Declaration. Palestinians were also becoming aware of their position, and were beginning to plan together and to make demonstrations. Najwa remembers that the British were ruthless at putting down the demonstrations.

During the Second World War, Najwa was a teacher in Haifa, Tiberias and Nazareth, and remembers a time of hard work with large classes of girls. She wrote plays and was active in the YWCA and the British Council. In 1947, when her father died, she was unable to take up a post as head of women's programmes in Palestinian Broadcasting because it was too difficult to move around. She wrote of what happened next.

> We were cut off from the world of the living and imprisoned in caves and camps, our condition deteriorating from one crisis to another . . . bewildered shocked, broken-hearted, humiliated . . . I saw one city after another attacked and occupied, one village after another wiped out . . . my people . . . becoming in one night refugees . . . What I felt most deeply was a sense of betrayal . . . my greatest pain came from fellow Christians who proclaimed that God's promises had been fulfilled . . . I felt that God had rejected us.

In 1950 Najwa married Rafiq Farah, an Anglican priest, and together they had a family and worked to build up the Arab Christian community. From 1950 to 1965 Najwa and Rafiq were also part and parcel of the Palestinian Arab Community. Many of Najwa's stories written at this time portray rejection and hopelessness. In 1965 Rafiq and Najwa moved through the Mandelbaum Gate to the West Bank, then under Jordanian rule. When the war of June 1967 came, followed by the subsequent occupation, Najwa recalls that it was like seeing a horror film twice over, 'as the planes were throwing bombs on the beautiful homes and their gardens of olive and fruit trees'. Najwa remembers a woman from Yalu who used to clean her house. The woman had elderly parents and one little girl who had polio and wore leg irons. The woman was given half an hour to clear her house before it was bulldozed.

In 1977 Rafiq and Najwa went to Beirut, where Syrian troops were keeping the 'peace' after the civil war of 1975. Najwa remembers that the city was physically very damaged and the people were spiritually very damaged. They stayed in Beirut for nine years, living opposite the hospital and watching a continuous stream of ambulances bringing the dead and injured in during the long years of continuous war. They gave unceasing help to those whose houses were damaged and they lived under almost constant insecurity and harassment until June 1982 when Israel invaded and they lived with daily death and suffering and then the 60-day siege. They finally left Beirut in 1986. Najwa remembers this leaving as very sad, for, 'in grief and sadness there is an involvement which normal living can never reach to or create . . . there is a relationship which is more binding, a discovery which is more revealing.' They moved on from a ministry of 40 years in the Arab Episcopal Church, to speak and write all over the UK. They now live with their family in Canada.

Najwa writes:

When I went to Britain and was asked to speak to groups about our Palestinian tragedy, the first thing I wanted to say to people was, 'Thank you for being willing to listen to us.' For years people expected us to say that the return and in-gathering of the Zionists in our country was God's fulfilment of his promises – even if that meant throwing out four million people from their own country.

If you go to the Holy Land and meet the local people, you will see with your own eyes that God is not a choosy God; he is not a land-divider; he is the creator of a continuously created/creative universe. With the coming of Jesus Christ, a new concept of God had been illuminated and revealed to us – a suffering God; a loving God; the power of love released into the world.

In the Church of the Holy Sepulchre we hope to ask forgiveness for all the children who were huddled in caves or camps and massacred; children whom Jesus would have had on his lap on the soft rolling hills of Galilee as he asked us all to be like them. He abhorred those who discarded his teachings of the spirit to cling to the letter of the law.

Nazareth people themselves do not ever forget that Jesus is their fellow-countryman. They are proud of the fact, but I do not think they do anything about it. They have no desire to perfect themselves. Certainly they are not more holy or more devout than any other people. Sometimes I used to feel that they have not changed, even from the times of Jesus. They are still provincial, unwilling to believe, and would say about any remarkable person – as they said about Jesus himself when he stood in their midst – 'Who is this? Isn't he the son of Joseph the carpenter?' Still, the people of Nazareth enjoy their Christianity.

For 17 years during our stay in our country, we saw thousands of tourists converging on the Holy land. Their agenda would comprise staying in posh hotels on the Jewish side of Jerusalem; being shown the holy places of modern Israel; rushing back to their planes with memories of the majestic stones and holy shrines, and with some touristy presents from the market and pictures taken with their cameras.

In 1992 we were in Denver, Colorado, with a gracious Anglican vicar and his wife. He made a tour to the Holy land with some Jewish friends. When we said, 'Did you go to St George's, the Anglican Cathedral on the West Bank? Did you meet any Christians?' he looked baffled. He never knew they existed.

We, on the other hand, would look at the thousands of tourists, especially those who come for Christmas, and gaze, surprised. We know we do not exist for them, though we also know that we have a role to play, a different and unique one. We are your liaison-officers, for we are rooted in the Middle East. We are full-fledged Arabs, proud of our heritage. We live with our Muslim brothers and sisters; share with them history, language, national aspirations and economic interests. We fight together the battles against ignorance for Arab awakening.

Reflection

The sky above is transparent blue.
Beyond, the lights of Kent glitter.
There is joy inexplicable
as a bird sings in a neighbourly tree.
Its rustling leaves evoke deep memories;
why this joy as the lights multiply?
They remind me of a carefree girl
who saw a landscape similar
of a lit horizon beckoning,
retained the memory of the magic
and dreamt of wondrous cities
where people of distinction dwell.
Would she ever reach such places
where dream-spun fabrics hang from above?

As dusk dims the backdrop of the sky
points of light strew the horizon
as with a myriad daffodils.
Twin rose-tinted trails of puff
articulated by a wandering plane;
strobe lights vying with the pulsing stars
frame the new-born crescent embroidered
on the blue indigo velvet of the heavens;
yet all is not the same for the one
who stands, bewitched by the perfect scene.
For her 'beyond' is here, and the future is the now.
For the wheel of time has spun;
a thousand days and nights are gone;
no glorious city had she seen.
Mortar and brick was what she found,
and people, strangers with new faces,
calculate with the same mind and
love to hate with uniform heart.
Is it true that what is lost is what we later wish for
and the magic we seek is far
beyond the shimmering time horizon?
With every sweeping swing, time's
pendulum carries us to the beyond
where our past is resting,
and magic lies in the memory
of a girl who had a dream.
But for now, let beauty reign
while the starlets wink and call.
Heedless is the wheel of time
as it spins its rythmic turn.
Now a moment is retrieved;
now a soul its joy regained.
For beyond the horizons a flame is lit
in deep oceans of mystery, defiant.
The thirst of wonder is never quenched.
Najwa Farah

Discussion and Action

Discuss some of the stereotypes we are tempted to create in order to understand the situation in the Middle East. Discuss how to avoid such an approach.

Find out more by meeting people from the Middle East. Perhaps make a visit, not to see the holy places but to meet the people there, the 'living stones'.

Khadijah

Najwa Farah

Mariam got married; her sister Khadijah did not. It was her lot to stay at home and care for her ageing parents, dreaming that one day she would get married, but nothing changed with the passage of time, and she no longer bothered, for another aspect of her personality had come to dominate her life: it was her whole dedication to Palestine. She showed great courage – like many women of her generation who found themselves locked in a camp after their villages had been destroyed by the Israeli army and they themselves thrown out. When siege or curfew was imposed on the camp, she was the one who dared sneak out of the camp, to bring bread and vegetables to those living there, exposing herself to be shot at by the occupying army.

When Mariam visited her father's home with her husband Bakr and their children she would leave all responsibility to Khadijah; she would sit comfortably on the old mat on the floor, stretch her legs and be careless about her children. It was up to Khadijah to run after them, to prepare a snack for them and teach them to sing of Palestine, while Mariam would make herself more comfortable, stretching herself on the straw bed, and would not move even when the children got out of control. 'Mariam! Order your children to stop screaming.' Mariam would not respond, she would even laugh, 'Take it easy. They are only children. Why don't you make us a cup of coffee', while she would change her position and sit cross-legged, her long embroidered dress covering her extremities. Mariam was fair-skinned, plump, easy-going, accepting things as they come; while Khadijah was dark, graceful and serious.

Their father would be sitting outside their one-room house in the alley of the camp, on the only old chair they had. Khadijah had embroidered two cushions to hide the worn parts in the seat and the back.

At the entrance she had planted in pots, mint, basil and parsley, and in the earth she planted tomatoes and spring onions. Most of the time there would be other men sitting with her father on little chairs in their sitting room and Khadijah loved to make coffee for the guests; it boosted her morale. In short, this little space in the alley, scented by the mint and basil, was their Garden of Eden, or was it?

It was not. Their lost Eden was somewhere else, for they came from Yalu, one of the three villages in the Latroun plain destroyed by Israel in the June war of 1967.

With a column of tanks the army moved into this strategic fertile plain where the famous Latroun convent lies, and in a few hours they destroyed the three villages of Yalu, Emmaus and Beit Nuba, throwing the owners of the land out. Khadijah's father owned an orchard in their village, Yalu. It had all the fruits that would grow in a Palestinian garden. They also grew their own vegetables and herbs. The house was in the midst of the orchard. '"Yallah barrah!*" they yelled at us,' Khadijah would tell the story of their exodus so many times. '"You have half an hour, then we are demolishing the house."' Khadijah would shiver whenever she repeated this tragic part of their exodus. After struggling to control herself and wipe the tears with the back of her hand she would try to continue her story in a more restrained manner. 'Half an hour – what can we pack in half an hour? What are we to leave? Our embroidered dresses! Provisions! Water for the journey ahead. My mother (God have mercy on her soul) would pick one item, put it back, pick another, throw it again, unable to decide on what is really important. We were not any better than her, we turned to my father. We did not find him – we realised that he was in the orchard, not concerned to carry anything with him, all he wanted was to be with his trees, bidding them

* Meaning 'Get out!'

68

farewell, singing dirges and crying.' Khadijah would repeat the dirges singing with a sad, low voice.

Doves that nest in my trees, keep an eye on my beloved.
From my own eyes carry my tears and water my damsels.

'Father, what are you doing here, come and help us, time is gone.'

'I want to be left to die here.'

'And leave us alone, three women roaming alone, no man to protect us?' But he went on addressing the olive trees:

'All my life, my head was lifted high up, I never begged. Why should I become a refugee while the enemy destroy my home?'

'What is the use of your dirges, Father, this is not the time for them.'

'I am carrying nothing. Leave me alone.'

It was no use, I ran inside to snatch his Abaya* and could hear him angrily threatening.

'But, by God – a day will come and we will be back. And the wound that is opened will be healed by a promised land.'

'By force we dragged my father and got him out to join the crowds heading towards Ramallah while the army was behind us driving us, lest any would come back.

'As we plodded on we were hearing the sound of guns and the noise of the destruction of the villages as the houses were collapsing after they planted the dynamite. It was then that my mother collapsed and died.' Here Khadijah would break down. The women who were listening to her would nod their heads several times, a sign that they knew what she was talking about and had been in a similar situation. As time passed Khadijah herself would compose new verses to

* A wide overcoat worn over men's traditional clothes

the lamentations of her father. Her neighbours also would contribute to the dirge repertoire, each lamenting their own destiny, perhaps lamenting an orchard like theirs.

Sometimes Mariam would shout Khadijah down: 'Stop, Khadijah! Should you always keep reminding us of the past, as if the present is not tragic enough?'

'By God, Mariam, your father laments his orchard, day and night, as if he is living with the trees he planted. Only yesterday he was telling me that his olive trees would have grown by now and come into fruition.'

Sarcastically Mariam comments, 'Poor Father, he does not know that they uprooted the trees and carried them, perhaps to an orchard of theirs.'

Two days later it was Mariam who came crying, afraid, seeking help and calling to her sister, 'Khadijah.'

'Mariam, what is it?'

'They have arrested my husband Bakr.'

'Why?'

'They claim he is accused of being a member of Fatah; he is now under administrative arrest. Suddenly they were around the house while he was coming back from work and they took him.'

After that, Mariam could not stay in her room alone. She was fearful for her children, so most of the time she slept at her father's house.

Days and nights passed and Bakr remained under house-arrest, not standing trial, like many hundreds of his own people.

It was no longer a strange gathering in the houses of the camp, where the ageing grandfather, the women and the children became the inhabitants of the humble homes of the refugees, without the young men who were detained.

Mariam went back to her old custom of visiting the neighbours and having coffee, while Khadijah was the one caring for the children, doing the chores of the house and caring for her old father. She always told the children about Palestine, and their village Yalu in the Latroun Plain.

The grandfather was pleased to have his grandsons around, especially Mustafa the older of the two. Mustafa was proud of his grandfather's orchard in Yalu and would tell his school friends about the orchard, and he would listen with great interest to the description of the house, the orchard, the different fruit trees, especially the new olive trees. He would dream of this lost paradise but he also believed that his return to it was imminent. Mustafa and his brother admired their grandfather who sat most of the time on the wicker chair outside their room and who was visited by the old men in the camp who listened to stories of happier days of Palestine.

There was the unhappy side of Mustafa's life, his father being under administrative arrest, but Mustafa did not know what that meant until one day he heard the men talking to his grandfather while he was serving them with coffee. One of the men was saying, 'We were relieved when my son was finished with the administrative arrest and became an ordinary prisoner, and we hope that Bakr's administrative arrest will also soon come to an end and that he will be transferred to an ordinary prison.' The man continued, 'Though a prison is a prison, one calamity is easier to cope with than the other.' Mustafa's grandfather soon became aware that his grandson was listening to this conversation and he hinted in a gesture to the visitor to change the subject.

The next day Mustafa learnt from his own friends what an 'administrative arrest' was and what his father could be suffering, being tortured under questioning. Likewise Mustafa had learnt not to make members of his family aware of what he knew and planned. He belongs to a group that calls itself the group for 'Defending and Freeing Palestine'. Mustafa is the assistant to the leader Mahmoud.

When the rains came it became much colder and their room in the camp was not kind to the old father, in spite of Khadijah's attempts to warm it with firewood that she had collected in the summer. The roof was leaking and she would put out buckets and containers that would hold the water

71

from the roof. The leaking was making different sounds with its repetitive dripping. The night was heavy for the old man, he would sit up panting and unable to breathe, and Khadijah would prepare camomile and aniseed. When the doctor in the camp came he was at his last breath.

The most distressed were Khadijah and Mustafa for they were so much attached to him; he was a symbol of that which was very deep in their lives. Mustafa used to be awake when his grandfather started to cough and breathe heavily and his mother would say to him, 'Lie down and sleep. You should not be the one to stay the night with your grandfather, you have school tomorrow,' and the grandfather would look at Mustafa and they would understand each other. 'Go to sleep, Mustafa, you have a great responsibility.' And Mustafa would say, 'I know, Grandfather.'

When Mustafa was at school, the grandfather died. His two daughters lamented with a loud voice and the women of the camp came in wearing their white scarves and singing their dirges. The neighbours brought chairs for the men to sit outside. Mustafa could not cry; he was very pale and silent. Khadijah was crying and saying, 'While my father was alive I was not afraid and did not feel our Palestine was lost. I felt it was with me, because he was Palestine to me, and now I was thrown out, lost, a refugee, and the orchard had gone'. The women would nod their heads, their scarves seeming like heaps of snow, agreeing to Khadijah's comments. One would say, 'True, whenever an old person dies a part of Palestine goes with him.'

As time passed the women visitors became fewer and fewer and Khadijah would speak as to herself, 'My father was the one who made me believe that we will return one day, and now who will assure me that this will happen?'

She heard a voice saying, 'I.' Khadijah was shaken, thinking she was speaking to her sister Mariam but she did not find her. It was Mustafa who was standing by the door listening to her lamentation. Khadijah realised that Mustafa had her feelings and with surprise said, 'You, my beloved, but you are still young; this is for grown men. '

Mustafa answered, 'The men are in prison; we are the ones who are left and a day for our return will come.' His mother on hearing him came in from outside, threatening Mustafa, 'Dare you move, Mustafa. It is enough that your father is in prison and your grandfather dead,' and she turned to Khadijah, scolding her, 'It is you who have broken the heart of the boy, because you weep for the orchard and the land, and indoctrinate the boy. As if Mustafa could fight the world. . . . Let the Arab nations fight, those who have the money, the men, the arms and the oil, or is it only that they talk and kiss each other whenever a plane lands, or are they expecting the children who are unarmed orphans with their fathers in prisons to bring victory to the Arab nation?'

She turned to Mustafa, 'You look after your studies and your younger brother; I do not want you to be involved, for your father is still under administrative arrest, and if you make any movement they will take their revenge on him, you understand!'

Although he understood what her words implied, Mustafa had other ideas. If his mother had some influence on him, the group he belonged to had a much bigger effect on him that outweighed his responsibility to his family. He could not go back on his vow. He is second to the leader and the motto is, 'Depend on oneself and not on the Arab Nation. '

There was a day when Mustafa, his leader, and his group would rise up and the Intifada would be the expression of their anger.

There were many demonstrations and the children of Palestine picked up stones from their land and used them to fight for Palestine.

There was a day when the army ran after the children of the camp and stones were thrown from near Khadijah's home, and she saw the army coming towards the house. She looked for Mustafa and saw the army holding a boy and striking him with the butts of their guns – it was Mustafa.

Khadijah and Mariam ran towards the army, fighting them to release Mustafa, and the solider was shouting at Khadijah, 'Get away from here or I will shoot you.'

'You shoot me!' and she threw her weight on to the solider trying to snatch the gun from him.

The women came with their white scarves surrounding the soldier, trying to save Mustafa while he was beating him, pulling his hair, and kicking him with his boots, and Mustafa was shouting, 'Auntie, go back; he will kill you.'

'No, I won't go back, I will fight him.' Now she was able to snatch Mustafa from the soldier with an inner strength she never thought she possessed. The soldier aimed his gun towards them. Khadijah stood facing the solider and shielding Mustafa, and the bullet came through her body, killing her, while Mustafa was pushed into an army truck to be taken to prison, and perhaps to face his father's fate.

The house again was filled with the women and the white scarves lamenting Khadijah with the same words that her father used:

But a day will come when the wound that bled
Will be healed by a hero that was promised.

The women would clap with one hand over the other and repeat, 'We shall return Khadijah, Intifada, Intifada', working themselves into a frenzy while repeating the word 'Intifada'.

Mariam would beat her breast, and with a new strength address the women, 'Khadijah would not like you to weep for her. She is a martyr, she is happy in paradise, because she died for Mustafa, for the bullet was directed at Mustafa.' A woman would say, 'We shall all miss her. She was the soul of the camp, especially since the Intifada, shielding the boys and hiding them from the army.'

Here Mariam turned to the women, saying, 'Never let Mustafa know that his aunt had died whilst he is in prison; he would be devastated, he might think that she was only wounded.'

As the last of the consolers left, Mariam embraced her second son while the night descended and the stars seemed as if they were pouring their light towards the camp, sympathising with its sorrows. The almond trees in the gardens like brides were standing with their white fluffy blooms.

Mariam was dreaming of her father, welcoming Khadijah to the gardens of Paradise and telling her that he spotted one like his orchard in Yalu.

Reflection

Reflect on what Khadijah went through in this story.

Olive Trees
Samir Mu'mmar

The Hills of Nazareth

Najwa Farah

A short story of endings and new beginnings from Najwa.
'Look ye at the lilies of the field how they grow.'

On one of the hills that overlook Nazareth there is a huge building. To reach it you have to climb its 108 steps. The steps are very broad: perhaps each step is 15 metres wide. When you reach the top exhausted and stand in the spacious area in front of the facade you are rewarded for your effort.

The landscape has a breathtaking splendour, the eye takes in the plain of Ibn Amer, where many a decisive battle took place. It looks so peaceful – a carpet of shades of green, gold and red. It is backed by ranges of hills, blue fading into a white that touches the horizon. The onlooker's heart is exalted, unable to comprehend what has aroused this joy. Is it nature, in all its exotic beauty? Is it the scent of the pine and the oak of the ancient majestic trees that rise high in the spacious area? Or is it the consequence of being faced with the tremendous reality that is Christianity, whose great legacy spread far and wide from these hills? The churches are everywhere, the inspiration that has awakened the hearts of many down through the ages, the different forms of monastic life are all indebted to the town below, where Jesus lived for 30 years. Jesus – perhaps he had sat here on this very spot, and certainly he saw what you are seeing. But it also occurs to you that it is not the huddled town below that lifts your thoughts up to the sublime; rather it is the hills on top of which you are seated that makes them soar. You can almost hear a voice, reminding you to heed the lilies of the field.

Turning to the building, you get the impression of looking at a medieval castle. It is surrounded by grounds that have been converted into playing fields, gardens and orchards. The tall ancient trees in front seem to stand there like guards; their rich scent and the slow movement of their branches in keeping with what was going on.

An atmosphere of sadness prevailed in the orphanage. The long service of its headmistress had come to an end. Her term of mission was finished; she had been recently notified by her mission headquarters that the time had come for her to retire, and so there she was, packing her belongings in her room. She was feigning courage and restraint in those last days, but now as she lifted her gaze from the wooden chest where she was carefully folding her clothes, her eyes fell on her mother's photograph which still hung on the wall. Her mother was still smiling to her calmly, as she had always done, especially when Doris was upset or afraid. The headmistress's mind went back to that moment when her mother helped her gently to her room while Doris sobbed aloud after reading her fiancé's name in the list of those killed in the Battle of the Marne. Her mother said then, 'You have to be brave and hold on to God. He will see you through. He will open a door for you.'

Even after the lapse of all those years Doris's heart would tremble when remembering that moment; a bottomless sadness pulled her downwards. The Marne! Time had laid a faded sadness on the very word, like the silent evening of an autumn day. Opposite her hill there is another; on which stands the Austrian Hospice. There is a wood and a cemetery where German soldiers lie. The crosses and their names are vivid to those who visit the cemetery. Strange how this should be the closest link to her Richard. Remembrance Day was the day when her feelings were upset the most.

And so it was that Doris stood and held on to God. A door opened to new horizons. She came out as a missionary headmistress to this orphanage. Twenty-five years had gone by since she first climbed the 108 stairs and saw the splendour of the view, with the town below, the plain and the mountains beyond. A great peace came over her; this is where she wanted to stay, to kneel in every spot, to thank God for calling her to his service . . . but these 25 years had gone, hurriedly: the wheel of time had turned with such speed that it seemed it had come to a full circle, with no consideration for her love for her work and for the children. She wasn't even aware of the white hairs on her head, nor the wrinkles in her face. . . . The letter that came out of the blue to advise her of her retirement reminded her of the government gazette that had listed the names of the dead; was it possible that there would be no life for her outside the orphanage, far away from this very spot? True, she had learnt that the Christian is a pilgrim in God's world, having to obey and accept difficulties with a welcoming heart, and 'God will open a door'. Of course – the door into the old people's home! She must not think like this; such thoughts were from the devil. With trembling hands she took down her mother's photograph – she stared at it intensely: 'Mother!' In a fleeting, terrible moment it seemed she heard her mother's voice: 'He will open a door.' She packed the photograph and put it in the chest. She felt lonely. The day came when the school gave a farewell party for the headmistress. The orphan girls sat in silent rows but their faces revealed their emotions: they had never known the orphanage without its headmistress, or the headmistress without the orphanage. They sang to her – school songs, and evening songs in the playground facing the plain, the scent of the pines reaching to them. They gave speeches and recited poetry. Then celebrities from the town spoke and praised her services and sacrifice; a girl from the top class presented her with an album. It had photographs of the town, the school buildings and the children's activities. She was followed by a little girl who gave her a bouquet of wild flowers, flowers from the Holy Land, from the hills around which she often walked with the children, especially in spring on a Sunday afternoon – the flowers that Jesus had seen and loved.

Then it was her turn to say something. She put on a smiling face . . . she spoke of a car that is coming to a very big bend not knowing what lies ahead, but trusting. God will guide her and show her what is round the bend.

Then it was all finished, including that last long night and the awful splendour of the dawn.

She found herself on a ship on her homeward journey, but her soul remained restless, anxious, in spite of her fervent prayers asking God to relieve her of her anxiety. She dreamed a lot; many of the dreams focused on her still being the headmistress and ministering to the school's needs.

She awoke one night, frightened. She dreamed that she had walked to the cemetery of the German soldiers on the opposite hill. One cross was illumined in a strange light. She read the text: 'Look ye at the lilies of the field how they grow.' Nearby stood a lily which she hadn't noticed before. It was budding, then full bloom, then it faded, its damaged petals fell on the ground, the wind blew the branches of the trees in the cemetery and bent them down; the cross continued to shine. When she turned to where the lily was, there was a bulb; it always grows in all its phases. What a strange dream!

Her eyes fell on her mother's photograph on the new wall in the very small flat which she rented. She watched the confident and relaxed face. It seemed more alive than hers.

There was a knock on the door. It seemed strange and remote, and it surprised her. She went to the door. Greatly relieved she recognised an old acquaintance, Jane. 'Sorry for coming without notice. I happened to be in London.'

'Please, come in, you're most welcome.'

'You must find it traumatic, coming back for retirement. You know I was in India and still feel lost. Everything has changed so much here.'

'Changed! Yes, it's not the England we knew. Would you like a cup of tea? I was about to have one.'

'How lovely. You prepare the tea – white linen tablecloth, nice china – and all that goes with it.'

'Yes.' To her friend Doris looked remote. Jane continued,

'Why don't you come down to Canterbury and spend a few days with me?'

'Thank you – that'll be nice.'

'Perhaps if you feel like it, there is a group of us who meet, very informally, and you can speak to us, tell us about Nazareth and the orphanage, and give us a message.' Doris nodded her head slowly. 'Please, do come and speak to us.'

'Thank you. I'll let you know.' She felt happy and she already had her theme.

Reflection 1

Bird of Grief

Bird of Grief, strange bird.
Did you visit me, and loved to stay?
Bird of Grief, when will you fly,
soar up to a far star?
Or is it you want to make my heart your home?
Isn't it time for you to depart
over surging seas exploring the unknown?
Will you leave, beautiful one,
and allow my heart to rest?
Will you leave today
and allow the bird of paradise to alight,
a nightingale that sang the dreams of my youth?

Najwa Farah

Discussion and Action

Najwa's story suggests that retirement may be dreaded because people no longer have an aim in life. Some people also lose their community when they stop working. Discuss disadvantages and advantages of retirement.

How may those who are not retired help?

Reflection 2 – A prayer from Germany

Herr, schicke was du willst,
  Lord, send what thou wilt –
ein Liebes oder Leides!
  pleasant things or unpleasant –
Ich bin vergnugt, dass beides
  I am content that both
aus deinen Handen quillt.
  flow from thy hands.

Wollest mit Freuden
  Do not overwhelm me
und wollest mit Leiden
  with joys or with sorrows!
mich nicht uberschutten!
  Gracious sufficiency
Doch in der Mitten
  lies in the middle.
liegt holdes Bescheiden.
Eduard Morike

The Slaves

Najwa Farah

The slaves have shadows,
dark shadows, stretching across the continents.
They write on the ground with their bent bodies.
They judge humanity,
pass their sentence . . .
They built the pyramids, the wall of China.
They push oars, become the food for the lions
to please emperors and crowds.
They sweat and thirst to water cotton plantations,
but the shackles have a clatter;
the clatter resounds in the air.
It is recorded, multiplies in the folds of the atmosphere.
It has echoes.
Generations will retrieve it
and they will hear in the ringing,
the groaning of the slaves,
of love, of hunger, sadness and separation.
The wind carries the groans the ghosts
pass across the continents,
laying their shadows on rising generations,
on history, on humanity.
The slaves are hungry.
There is rebellion.
Slaves have hearts.
They are human.
Lift your hands off the slave.
Allow the dawn to proceed.

A Poet Who Loved the Poor

Najwa Farah

Grief has gnawed at your heart.
No solace came from the nocturne gardens of sorrow,
though the sailing moon was a sympathiser.
In circles she is still roaming, looking for someone
who would deliver the message.
The night as well had become an ally,
responding to your anguished question,
a witness to the crimes committed behind its black curtain,
in the camps where Palestinians live their bondage,
where blood and suffering reign.
Also in the quarters of the Sullan and Lilaki,
and the squares of a city that was fair and joyful,
for the dreams of the defeated are trampled
by the stealthy steps of death.

Will the poet's fascination with love, beauty, and truth
be ever exhausted?
O my poet, anguish shall reveal your secret
and so will the nocturnal gardens of sorrow.
Your unanswered question will still be echoed.
Will the rising generations ever stand for the poor
as you have done in your short life,
and died for the cause?
The sun and the moon will still alternate in the sky
and the day will follow the night.
Will ever the change in this unexplained cosmos take place?
As for me, I shall lay a wreath of lilac on your grave,
there in a northern spot under an oak tree
in a country that embraces heaven.

Open House

The Open House peace centre is in Ramle, Israel. The history of the house is remarkable and so encouraging in an environment where people have come to fear each other. Dahlia Landau arrived in Ramle in 1948 from Bulgaria with her family. They were one of many Jewish families who came to Israel at this time, often from suffering situations all over the world. Dahlia was a baby then and grew up in Ramle in a beautiful and empty Arab house. In 1967 she was at home when three Arab men called, including Bashir Al-Khayri, who had been born in the house and forced to leave when Israel was formed, when he was 6 years old in 1948. Bashir could return to visit his old home in 1967 because the West Bank had been occupied by Israel. His family grew to know Dahlia and her family, and, as the years passed, and Dahlia inherited the house from her parents and married Yeheskal Landau, the right way forward emerged – the 'Open House' where Christian, Muslim and Jewish people may meet and share and learn to develop trust.

Open House began in 1991, and now includes classes for children, a day care centre for babies, a place for Arab/Jewish reconciliation work, a peace camp, and much more.

Neve Shalom/Wahat al-Salaam

Neve Shalom/Wahat al-Salaam means 'Oasis of Peace'. It is a community which aims to develop understanding and respect between Jews and Muslim and Christian Palestinians. It was formed in 1972, high on a hill overlooking the Vale of Ayalon in an area with a long history of struggle and war stretching back to the days of Joshua.

The community offers programmes of meeting and working together for the people at every stage in their lives. There is also a school for peace. The meetings between the people are sometimes traumatic, for it is hard for a Palestinian to meet a Jew who will one day enter the Israeli army, and it is hard for a Jew to meet a Palestinian who is working to evict his people from settlements they have built through their own hard work. The hope is that in the meetings some of the ignorance and fear may be broken, that there may be the beginning of change.

Reflection 1

Once we realise that our own path to religious fulfilment is not at odds with our neighbour's, that we are both beloved of God and can serve the Divine in equally blessed ways despite our different theologies . . . then our passion will enhance our faith, not corrupt and destroy it. And we can serve as examples to others who are also struggling, in good faith, to express their passionate devotion to the Creator and the creation. *Yeheskel Landau*

Discussion and Action

1. Discuss what both Dahlia and Bashir's families most probably had to go through to come to the 'Open House' of meeting and sharing.

2. Where is there a possibility of 'Open House' in our neighbourhood? What may we learn from Open House and Neve Shalom/Wahat al-Salaam towards breaking down ignorance and fear at home?

Reflection 2

While the Jewish people were scattered throughout the world they often had to travel long distances to visit a grave.

At each visit a stone would be left to show that the visit had been made and the dead had been remembered.

Although this practice was not traditionally found in Israel, it is now followed at Yad Vashem, the memorial to the Holocaust in West Jerusalem. Stones are piled up around a statue of a grieving woman to show that visitors have remembered those who died in the Holocaust.

Discussion and Action

The twentieth century witnessed many atrocities. Share possible ways of remembering those who have died, whilst at the same time working for a peaceful and just future.

A Prayer for Jerusalem

Najwa Farah

Our heavenly Father,
    who allowed us to live in this city
    where your beloved Son was crucified
    and raised from the dead,
    make us worthy of its heavenly message.
We pray that the holy places will turn us
    to the things that deepen our faith
    and renew in us the hope of everlasting life.

We beseech you, Lord,
    who know what the people of all faiths in this holy city
    have suffered, and are suffering:
    uprootedness, lostness,
    the pain of being torn apart in separation,
    the pain of unsettlement,
    the pain of death.
We beseech you, Lord, to give this holy city
    peace built on justice.
We beseech you, Lord, to give the people of this city
    calm in their souls and courage in their hearts.
Strengthen, O God, the hearts of those of all faiths
    who work to bring justice.
Help us, God, as we pass through difficult trials,
    that we may grow to know your truth
    and that we may witness to you by our lives.

May the way of the cross be the one that we choose
    for ourselves,
    that each of us may carry his cross to follow you,
    Shepherd of our souls.

Amen.

The Jerusalem Princess Basma Centre

The Princess Basma Centre is named after a Jordanian princess and is a rehabilitation and education centre for disabled children on the Mount of Olives in East Jerusalem. There are also branches in the West Bank. Muslims and Christians work side by side in the Centre, which was set up in 1959 to care for victims of polio, cerebral palsy, muscular dystrophy and disabilities due to injury. The hope of the centre is that children will become as independent as possible. Parents are trained to help the children when they go home, supported by a community-based rehabilitation team.

Mohammed's Story

Mohammed lives with his grandfather, parents and two brothers. He has spina bifida and cannot walk. He has no toys at home, and only a pile of sand in the street outside. His father is ill and cannot work, and the house is small. Mohammed enjoys drawing pictures with a lot of blue sky. He will go to school when he gets his wheelchair. He enjoys going out with his grandfather, when he sits on a horse, in a special box.

Nisreen's Story

Nisreen is an 8-year-old Bedouin girl who lives in a tent with her parents and a brother and sister. They are a poor family. They sleep on mattresses on the floor of the tent. There are many other members of the family in the camp which is ten kilometres from the nearest village. Every two weeks Nisreen's father has to drive a water tank into the village to collect the water for all the people in the camp. Nisreen's family keeps sheep and goats for meat and milk, and they sell the wool. Nisreen had a badly twisted foot and spent a long time in the Centre, so that it could be straightened. She was visited by her grandmother, an old lady dressed in black and with tattoos on her forehead. Nisreen loves her. When Nisreen's foot had healed after the operation, she was given surgical boots, leg braces and a walking frame so that she could walk a little. She also joined a special education class at the Centre, and could go on to a regular school if she did not live in such a remote desert area. There is a taxi, but it is expensive and does not operate in the winter. Nisreen says that her home is surrounded by the desert, but when the rain comes there are wild flowers.

Coptic Crosses

The Copts are the native Christians of Egypt and the direct descendants of the ancient Egyptians. The term 'Coptic' is derived from the Greek word *Aigyptos*, meaning Egyptian.

'Out of Egypt have I called my son' (Matthew 2:15). A special blessing was conferred on Egypt as Jesus spent his early childhood in this land and is said to have travelled from Sinai in the East to the Nitrian valley in the West, and southwards to Assiut, the heart of Upper Egypt. Egypt was always a land of refuge, especially in times of famine. Joseph lived in Egypt. Jacob and his sons visited.

St Mark, the writer of the second Gospel, was the founder of the first African Christian Church in Alexandria in the year 42 CE. He ordained priests and deacons, and was martyred in 68 CE. He is considered the first in the unbroken line of Patriarchs of the Coptic Church. His Holiness Pope Shenouda III is the 117th Pope of Alexandria. The growth of the Church in Egypt has been accompanied by 'waves of persecution'. After many disputes the Church is now recognised as 'miaphysite', which means that it recognises both natures of Jesus Christ, being joined inseparably in the 'One Nature of God the Logos Incarnate'. Nevertheless, the Church did not avoid isolation and some persecution, because it was seen, until the twentieth century, as 'monophysite'.

The seventh-century Arab invasion of Egypt led to four centuries of peace and development for the Copts, and it was not until the second millennium that the Copts began to be restricted. After that Islam gradually gained precedence.

Monasticism began in the Coptic Church in the third century and flourished in the fourth century, with the birth of hundreds of monasteries. Some monks were hermits, some lived alone and gathered together occasionally, and some lived a community life.

The Copts number about five million in Egypt. There are

some fifty thousand in Sudan and several hundred in Jerusalem and Palestine as well as in other Middle Eastern countries. There are Coptic students and families living in Europe, America and Australia.

Bahga El Raheb

Bahga El Raheb died in June 1999. She was an active member of the Coptic Orthodox Church until two weeks before she died. Her life was spent in striving for human rights, in Egypt and around the world. She had a special concern for the development and well-being of women and girls. Her writing here brings out her frustration that women did not always take the opportunities open to them in her generation, and in younger generations also. She did research into the tradition of women deaconesses in her church which resulted in ordinations in 1979, but sadly this was not continued in most dioceses.

Her writing on the imprisonment of priests and others, before and after the assassination of President Sadat in 1981, is vivid and brings out her bravery. She demanded the right to visit the prisoners and to take food.

She worked in the office of Pope Shenouda III for many years and was head of the Women's Division of the Socialist Labour Party in Egypt. She was one of the founders of the Arab Women's Solidarity Association and was thus a pioneer in bringing Christian and Muslim women together. She attended many international conferences, always working and appealing for human rights and especially for the rights of women. She was a campaigner for the Decade in Solidarity with Women. She spoke at many conferences, always committed to work for human rights. She was ever challenging and ever friendly. I will always remember the warm welcomes I received at her home in Ealing, her generous food and conversation and her love of her church and people. She writes here about Coptic women and about the struggle for human rights in Egypt.

Coptic Women: Agents of Change

Bahga El Raheb

A strong movement towards change and empowerment had already started in Egypt, in the wake of the national revolution in 1952. Coptic women, as a part of the whole Egyptian society, sought change.

It was hard for me to persuade church leaders at that time to establish our very first Coptic Hostel for university girls from all over Egypt to study in Cairo. At last, a hostel was founded in Giza in October 1951. I remember how much I suffered until it became a reality. It was the same when I was founding the first Christian Children's Club at Tanta, 1952 to 1955.

Thank God there are now many hostels for Coptic girls in most of the colleges supervised by churches; also youth clubs and development centres. I met the same problems again when establishing the first governmental hostel for girls in Banha, 1961 to 1965.

There has only been one Egyptian woman historian in this present century, a Copt by the name of Iris El-Masri, who died in 1995. The first woman to graduate in medicine was Helena Sidaros.

In 1975, the International Year for Women, I managed, with the support of His Holiness Pope Shenouda III, Pope of the Coptic Orthodox Church, to persuade our church hierarchy that Coptic women have to be aware of and actively concerned with global issues. Our first effort was a conference held for Coptic women, to help them to become more informed and involved in the social, cultural, spiritual and political realities of the world.

In this same year, His Holiness Pope Shenouda appointed a woman teacher, Nagwa El-Ghazali, at the theological college in Cairo, and he chose three women to attend and take part in a Middle Eastern Council of Churches conference in Brummana, Lebanon.

We began a really blessed era as Coptic women. In 1979 I was assigned, as a student of the Higher Institute for Pastoral Care, to do research on deaconesses. I spent two weeks in the British Library to discover the oldest tradition of the Church of Alexandria. Twenty-seven deaconesses were ordained for Cairo, and then the conflicts began.

Is it ordination or consecration?

That was the end of it. Some bishops said, 'No! Women can only be nuns!' Others said that women should only be consecrated as lay people, in celibacy. This is an example of the huge gap between the Pope and most members of his Holy Synod, amongst whom some are still 'anti-women'; an attitude influenced by the whole culture of our society. Only a few bishops were willing to give their talented, bright women the opportunity to share in all areas of church activity for their own personal growth and the development of their communities.

I consider the period 1980 to 1985 one of the worst eras of our country's history, and of the Coptic Church. The strange, violent, extreme trends and fundamentalist tendencies began to strengthen, and my own struggle had to take another form.

Since 1978 I had worked along with the honourable members of the Opposition, the Socialist Labour party. I was head of the Women's Branch. This was the legal channel for my struggle, although very few Copts took an active part in politics. This was a result of a philosophy of not putting ourselves into temptation and troubles, and thinking it wiser to stay away from conflicts until the storms passed. Indeed, the violence escalated and the corruption was becoming very scary. Moral values began to disintegrate. I joined the Arab Organisation of Human Rights and was one of the founders of the Arab Women's Solidarity Association (AWSA). Pope Shenouda III was placed under house arrest by President Sadat, who was assassinated by Muslim extremists just 40 days after he had imprisoned 1,500 very active leading Egyptian intellectuals, amongst whom were eight bishops and ten priests. We went through a very difficult and dangerous time, a time I detail later.

As the late 1970s had marked progress for Coptic women, so the end of the 1980s seemed to mark stalemate. In 1989, there were two gatherings I attended where I discovered that Coptic representation was insufficient. I came to the conclusion that either the leaders of our Church felt themselves to be self-sufficient, or other Churches do not know much about us, or both. These gatherings were, firstly, the Orthodox Conference held by the World Council of Churches in Crete, in preparation for the Canberra conference in 1991. The other was the All-Africa Council of Churches held in Lome, Togo, and attended by 300 women of whom I was the only Orthodox woman.

I was particularly shocked, knowing that within the women's decade, the Orthodox Church of Egypt was represented by eight bishops led by the Pope himself, with only one woman who was accompanying her husband, a Coptic priest. That was the size of the delegation of the Coptic Orthodox Church to the WCC Sixth Assembly in Canberra, Australia, in 1991.

Another shock was the realisation that women themselves do not care. Even when they know their rights, they are not very keen on gaining them, nor are they willing to strive for them. I believe that patriarchal attitudes have kept women as second-class citizens, ill-equipped to realise their potential role, or to participate fully in social, economic, political and religious life. I had hope in my own Church, but now I feel that we Coptic women have not entered the twenty-first century as fully empowered citizens.

I chose to be away from my country, Egypt, leaving everything – the Women's Desk at the Patriarchate, the Socialist Labour Party, my home, all my activities, for a while. ENOUGH IS ENOUGH! It was my own personal choice.

We lost all sense of justice; we lost all peace; we spoilt

the environment. We are going back hundreds of years. Our intellectuals are leaving the country. Our young people emigrate. Violence is escalating. Writers and artists are being murdered. Most of my Muslim colleagues are hiding behind their veils as if, in the past, they were not religious. There are challenges from inside and outside. Churches are being burnt, rights violated.

The Copts will never complain or revolt. We love our land and our Church. We have been under pressure all through our history.

I came to live in the United Kingdom, hoping to find a better view of human rights in a country that claims it is seeking to provide justice and peace for its people and for thousands of refugees.

Renewed vision

In 1992, I glimpsed hope for a better future as I led a workshop on women in the Middle East, at the Anglican Encounter, at Bahia, Brazil. There, I was impressed to see native Americans from the north and the south, speaking bravely about their plight; very spiritual, very humane, as they discussed their hopes and fears. I said in my heart, 'One day, there *will* be peace and justice!'

I must now renew my hope and faith, forget the past and look forward to a world where peace and human rights are recognised by all.

Tears That Can Never Be Forgotton

Bahga El Raheb

Like all Christian Copts, I followed, for ten years, a peaceful
and silent approach to protest against the ongoing and painful,
progressing tide of unjustified persecution, hardships (such
as I personally suffered in my professional life), and massacres
against Copts. I spent this decade struggling through all the
available legal channels.

At that time, 1978-1989, I was the head of the Women's
Division of the Socialist Labour Party of Egypt, and one of the
twenty founders of the Arab Women's Solidarity Association,
also a member of the Arab organisation for Human Rights.
One of my most painful experiences was going through the
process of elections for our parliament in 1984 and 1987. I
was at the top of the list of my party in one of the biggest
Cairo boroughs, in spite of the ever-present reality of the
existence of the most powerful opposition.

One of many incidents during this era was my visit to the
prison where eight of our bishops and 24 priests were
imprisoned during the time of Sadat. President Sadat gave
his orders to arrest 1,500 people, amongst whom were heads
of political parties, writers, church leaders, Muslim leaders
and human rights activisits. Pope Shenouda III was placed
under house arrest alone, in a separated area in the region of
St Bishoy's monastery. Eight bishops and 24 priests were
amongst 135 Copts who were arrested. One Catholic and
one Protestant were arrested and they were released before
the others.

It was said that Sadat 'arrested the mind of Egypt', for
the most active intellectual leaders, both men and women, in
all areas, were imprisoned. Father Zakaria Botros, who was
expelled from Egypt, and is now serving our Coptic Church
in Brighton in the UK, was arrested on 3 September 1981, and

released after 318 days. For 44 days these people were kept three to a cell measuring 180 centimetres by 160 centimetres, with a hole of 50 centimetres for a toilet, and an opening of 10 by 10 centimetres in the door.

President Sadat was assassinated on 6 October 1981, less than 40 days after his decree. After his death, these people were all moved on to different prisons. The Coptic prisoners, including the clergy, were moved to the Margue prison in the eastern part of Cairo.

When President Mubarak came into power, he decreed that all political prisoners should be released. First, they had to gather to meet him at his residence in Heliopolis. With this group were seven leaders of my Socialist Labour Party. Mubarak refused to discuss anything concerning the Copts for a long time. Still, the miracle of the death of Sadat had left the Coptic Christians with hope and trust in God. Soon, they were permitted to visit the Pope, but only with the approval of the Secret Service of the Security Department. I was not allowed to visit for three years, until 3 October 1984, just two months before His Holiness was released and permitted to pray at Christmas on 7 January 1985.

By God's grace, I had the chance to visit the prison in Margue twice, in order to discuss the curriculum of Christian books with one of the bishops, who was an author of books for the three stages of education. This was planned by the Minister of Education during the first parliament of Mubarak's rule. The Minister asked the opposing parties to share in developing and changing the education system; the subjects and programmes, and one of them was Religion, and the books used for teaching. I was assigned to do this job for my Party, and the research was approved by the Party.

I asked the officer of the Security Department for permission to visit the prison. He demanded written confirmation from 'the Papal Committee which was assigned by Sadat and rejected by the Copts'. I brought it for him, but he then asked for the approval of my Party, and the leader of my Party gave me what I asked for, but, instead of taking it to the officer, I went directly to the prison with the two letters of approval.

Just after the soldier at the gate took me to the Governor's office, and before introducing myself to him, I found Bishop Beimen sitting relaxing in the big office, and with his laughing sense of humour, he greeted me with the words, 'Hello, Joy!' (He was the first one to call me Joy, which is the English translation of my name, Bahga.) Before I had a chance to speak, there entered two priests; one of them was Father Zakaria Botros.

Thank God I had enough time to tell them my news. Both the leader of our Socialist Labour Party, and Dr Hilumy Murad, a former Minster of Education and former Dean of Ain Shams University who had also worked for the UN and who was a friend of the Pope, who had been imprisoned with them – both these men would meet President Mubarak the same week.

The Mayor ordered tea for me while he had to finish with a case, as he told me. That 'case' was the wife of Father Tadros Yacoub, asking permission for her brother, who had just arrived from Saudi Arabia, to visit Father Tadros, her husband.

The Mayor ordered a soldier to go and bring the prisoner. For my part, I meant not to show that they were friends of mine. Father Tadros is a theologian who served in Alexandria, then in Australia and California.

On entering the office, Father Tadros found his wife standing on one side of the Mayor's desk, and me sitting on the other side in silence. With a face full of sadness, he looked at his wife, Mary, without a word, while she was just about begging the Mayor to permit her brother to come in, repeating that he was in a taxi outside the gates of the prison and coming directly from the airport. I wanted to stand up, out of respect. I couldn't swallow my tea, my heartbeats surely could be heard! Mary was so strong. She didn't weep, but Father Tadros, who was not looking at the Mayor, kept looking at her, very calm, very kind, with tears . . . My priests, the most refined, gentle, meek persons – prisoners, and being treated as criminals!

The room at last became silent, with a sad, sad silence . . . I couldn't help it! I got to my feet, told the Mayor that I would come again the next day. I showed him the two letters, telling him that I was in the process of getting him the approval he needed. I went out weeping. On the way, I saw some of the other priests but I couldn't shake hands. I didn't want to reveal that I knew them. The rules were that a soldier had to accompany me to the outside gate.

The next day, I went to the officer, and, to my astonishment, he told me that he needed the approval of the General Prosecutor. I went directly, but his office told me he would not approve such a visit. I went again to the prison, saw the Governor, told him that I had already handed in the letters of permission so could he please call the office on the telephone and ask for the permission. I was shaking and scared, but what I had hoped was to meet Bishop Beimen who was, to my relief, in the office again, sitting in the same chair. I was able to tell him that prayers were being said in all our churches, and a very big effort was being made within all political and religious national and international organisations for their release. I had to tell him that I was blacklisted and not permitted to visit His Holiness, so I needed their prayers too.

I know that the officer told the Governor that there was no need for me to contact anybody, but I know that my visit was a comfort for them, and a big relief for me. I know that, afterwards, a van of food and medicine, each time carrying the Korban (bread and wine) for the Eucharist, was permitted every week for the prisoners. They said Mass daily in the prison. Even the Mayor asked for their prayers for his three children who fell sick at one time. He had faith in their prayers. He said clearly, 'I heard you every day crying, "Kirie Eleison" until the man was dead. You can pray for anything and it will be done.'

Coptic Prayer for the Beginning of the Day

To thee, O Master that lovest all men,
    I hasten on rising from sleep;
    by thy mercy I go forth to do thy work,
    and I pray to thee:
    help me at all times, in everything;
    deliver me from every evil thing of this world
    and from every attack of the devil;
    save me and bring me to thine eternal Kingdom.
For thou art my Creator,
    the Giver and Provider of everything good;
    in thee is all my hope,
    and to thee I ascribe glory, now and ever,
    and to the ages of ages.
Amen.

Attributed to St Macarius of Egypt

Reflection

The Coptic cross is made into many hundreds of shapes by the plaiting of pieces of leather. The cross is made during meditation on the interweaving of the cross of Christ into the world. The Church can never exist in isolation from the world but must always be part of the world, even if that means struggle and suffering.

In the Coptic tradition, the Eucharistic bread is always round, symbolising the beloved universe. In the middle of the bread is one big cross symbolising the Christ, surrounded by twelve crosses, symbolising the apostles.

The priests who were in prison must have been very frustrated, knowing how much they were needed by their country and people, who were also suffering.

Discussion and Action

1. Bahga showed her solidarity with those who were in prison, and gave them new life and hope. Where might solidarity be shown at the beginning of the twenty-first century in our communities?

2. Is it possible for brave pioneers for human rights to spread their commitment to a wider group, and so to become more effective agents for change and justice? Think of examples.

3. Read the United Nations Declaration on Human Rights, and discuss its implications.

4. Do you agree with Bahga that some women and girls do not wish to take advantage of the education and other opportunities that are open to them in the modern world? How can attitudes be changed?

A Coptic Cross

RODRIGUES ISLAND
INDIAN OCEAN

Introduction

Rodrigues is an isolated island in the Indian Ocean, 350 miles from the nearest land, which is Mauritius to the west – and Mauritius is not much bigger! Thousands of miles of lonely ocean surround tiny Rogrigues. The first settlers in 1691 were Huguenot refugees fleeing persecution in France. They left after two years of lonely colonisation and never came back.

Until recently there were very few roads, no electricity and a very fragile water pipeline. Electricity came to the island in the early 1970s. The water supply is still fragile. In September 1996 it was announced that the island was about to get the very first direct (live) TV news programme from Mauritius!

Rodrigues has a population of around 35,000 people, mostly of African descent and mostly engaged in farming or fishing, or both, and the little island is way behind Mauritius in the economic and industrial development of recent years.

Four friends started the Craft Aid Rehabilitation and Production Centre in Rose Hill, Mauritius, in 1982. This enterprise soon proved to be very successful and the directors decided, in 1987, to share this success with Rodrigues, where they planned to open a small, subcontracting branch. It was hoped that this would involve a few of the 700 handicapped persons on Rodrigues.

When Paul Draper was commissioned to go to Rodrigues and start up the project in 1989, it soon became clear that a much more extensive project than that originally planned could be established there. For one thing, there was no special provision in schools for children with any sort of handicap. There was no training centre. Even basic medical care was less developed than in Mauritius. Many cases had to be sent across the sea to hospitals in Mauritius. It became clear that planning for the situation on Rodrigues needed to be long-term, and carefully thought through.

Today, the same kind of dynamic progress made by Craft Aid in Mauritius is beginning to be seen in Rodrigues.

Craft Aid, Rodrigues Island

Paul Draper

The Gonzague Pierre Louis Special Learning Centre was started in 1994, and named in honour of a local blind person (see story below) in response to a need for such a school. I found around 100 handicapped children on Rodrigues. Sending all these children to Mauritius, to the special centres there, was not a practical possibility for many reasons. Most of them did not attend school at all and just stayed at home, living in a restricted world of isolation and deprivation. Those who did go to school merely sat in classes without any special help, and making little progress.

It was decided to start off by specialising in children with hearing impairment. Up to 30 children were identified on Rodrigues, between the ages of two and twelve. With help from organisations overseas, the centre was built and equipped and a daily programme was started. All the children first identified were catered for and new ones joined the programme, so the programme started with about 40 children. They are all supplied with hearing aids and are learning to communicate through speech. Sign language is unknown on Rodrigues.

Some of the children who are managing in normal school with back-up from the Centre are visited regularly by staff members in their schools and also their families. In this way, they are encouraged and their progress is monitored. Extra practical help, such as food and clothes, is given to children who come from very poor homes, or where there has been some particular tragedy (see the story of Claudino Ernest, below). Providing food helps to ensure that the children arrive at the Centre nourished, so that they do not faint on the way, or fail to keep going until mid-afternoon when they have to start the long trek home. None of the children lives near the centre. Their homes are spread out over the four corners of the island in isolated hamlets far from roads.

In the Craft Aid workshop there are three departments. One makes jewellery, which is exported to agencies in Europe, from polished pieces of coconut; there is a furniture-making department, and a group which makes chain-link fencing. These latter are all sold locally.

But the pride and joy of Craft Aid Rodrigues is the honey! Rodrigues honey is famous. It won a silver medal at the National Honey Show in London in 1994. They have their own hives and also their own processing and bottling department. Honey is exported in bottles to Mauritius, where it finds its way on to the breakfast tables at the big hotels, and on to the shelves of the local supermarkets and stores.

The Craft Aid workshop building is new; in fact, it is not yet completed. It will be some time before all the buildings are completed. There are also plans to extend the work of the special education centre to the visually impaired.

The Inspiration of Gonzague Pierre Louis

Gonzague Pierre Louis lives in a valley. To get from his house to the main road takes a stiff, uphill walk of one hour. In the rain, it is very slippery. For most people, this would be a walk to do a few times a year only (the fewer the better) but Gonzague has to do it every day, there and back. Yet he loves it. Why? Because he goes off to work, daily, and he is glad! He has to get up at 5 am, and he likes that too! How can anyone actually like so many inconvenient and rather unpleasant things?

The reason is this: Gonzague is blind. For years he sat in his house down in the valley with nothing to do. He has been blind from the age of 9 and there was just nothing for him to do, either at home or nearby. At least, no one could suggest anything. He did receive a small government disability pension but it was mainly his wife who did the planting and sold handicraft items to eke out a living.

In 1989, Craft Aid in Mauritius decided to open a rehabilitation and production workshop on Rodrigues. For the first time in his life Gonzague had the chance of a regular job which he enjoyed – making coconut jewellery and woodworking under supervision – and able to earn a regular wage. Gonzague can put up with the inconveniences and even his blindness in order to take advantage of the opportunity and improve life for himself and his family.

The money he earns has been used to improve his house and help feed and clothe his children. He is never late for work; never absent. He works hard and well. He is an inspiration to all.

Gonzague has now had some of the songs he has written recorded on cassette.

Drama in the Family of Claudino Ernest

Dramatic events in the lives of people do not occur, as they do in TV soap operas like *Dallas* or *Dynasty*, just to the wealthy and powerful people who seem to have more money than sense. Sometimes, acute drama comes to poor, simple village people living far away from the big cities of developed countries. Here, on the remote Indian Ocean island of Rodrigues, we are face to face with a big, tragic drama in the life of one of our handicapped children who comes to the Centre we run for special education for the hearing-impaired.

Claudino Ernest is 13 years old. He is hearing-impaired (deaf mute) and he lives in a small, tin shack with his family, which is connected to other habitations in the quiet countryside by a simple track. There is no road and no vehicles.

There is just the sound of the wind and the far-off roar of the sea on the coral reef.

His family is poor, like so many Rodriguan families. The people of Rodrigues have always, since the island was first populated by freed slaves of African descent from Mauritius about 200 years ago, scraped a meagre existence from the land growing maize and keeping a few cattle and poultry.

There are a few other families in the grouping of shacks on the hillside. The people are mostly related to one another, and all share a common, hard lot in life. We have visited the family of Claudino several times and taken food and clothing to help eke out the family budget. The most important role we have, however, is to make sure that Claudino wears his hearing aid and comes to our Centre as often as possible. To be frank, he is not one of our success stories. He rejects the hearing aid and rarely comes to the Centre. However, through our contact with him, we discovered that his cousin has quite a severe physical handicap. He now works daily at the Craft Aid workshop and has learned to make coconut jewellery. He is one of the production team in this section.

We also noticed that there was only one pair of 'savattes' (rubber sandals) between all the members of the family. We bought them one pair each so that each person has something to put on their feet. Now, they no longer have to walk around in the mud and dirt barefoot, picking up infections and worm larvae.

The father of the family used to go off each day to join a fishing group on another coast of the island and bring home fish which the family would cook. Other than that, the only regular income is the old-age pension of the grandma.

It was while he was away fishing that the father got involved with another woman who lived near to where they kept the boat. One day, a drama developed which ended with the man stabbing this other woman, and, in a passionate rage, he returned to his home and hanged himself. The woman died a few days later. Two people dead and a family left with disgrace and the loss of the only breadwinner. It was a very sad and demoralised family that we visited with a few items of support a few days after these events.

Just a week later, Claudino's mother gave birth to another baby, a daughter. Another mouth to feed, less income to buy food as well as the recent tragedy to deal with. However, through all this turmoil, the family remained intact and our support for them goes on.

The Story of Glenford

Inside Craft Aid, Rodrigues, we offer the education, rehabilitation and employment of young people with disabilities, so that they feel as 'normal' as possible in life. Take Glenford, for instance, who attends the Rodrigues special learning centre, the Centre Gonzague Pierre Louis. His life could not have started in a more abnormal fashion. He was orphaned and became a street kid.

Yes, even in Rodrigues there are kids who live on the street with apparently no home to go to. Not many, it is true, but it does happen. Begging from shop to shop and spending the night sleeping in cartons on the quayside, Glenford was more obvious than other ragged urchins because he could not hear or speak.

Several times he was brought along to our Centre, but he enjoyed his free life of begging and wandering around, fishing or swimming in the warm sea whenever he felt like it. He never went hungry as people generally are kind. They used to feed him and give him a few rupees to spend. He could not see any reason for complicating his life with things like school, let alone the bother of wearing a hearing aid.

However, eventually he was picked up by the police for suspected thieving. It was at this point that the Aukbar family of Mangues offered to take him in and give him a home. Judy Aukbar is the secretary at the Rodrigues Association for the Disabled, and she was aware of Glenford's plight. She persuaded her mother that one extra burden would make little difference. Glenford (or Koontay to his friends) has settled in well to a welcoming home and a loving family who ensure that he comes regularly to our Centre, is clean and cared-for, and – very importantly – wears his hearing aid. He is a very bright boy. Because he has few inhibitions, he is learning to talk and understand speech, thanks to his hearing aid. He is now being fitted with a new and better 'behind the ear' aid which will make him even more 'normal', and able to cope with life. Now, we just need to find out if he has a birth certificate!

Altogether, 25 children with impaired hearing form part of the programme at the Centre Gonzague Pierre Louis, which is administered by the Trevor Huddleston House Association part of the Craft Aid set-up. All of these children will qualify for job-training in the Craft Aid workshop which was built in 1995, next to Trevor Huddleston House.

All the children enjoy weekly visits, started by the Revd Jean Paul Solo, for a Christian song and time of reflection each Monday. This tradition is maintained by Brian and Claudette Adeline and is much enjoyed by all at Craft Aid, Rodrigues.

Reflection 1

You are the caller
You are the poor
You are the stranger at my door

You are the wanderer
The unfed
You are the homeless
With no bed

You are the man
Driven insane
You are the child
Crying in pain

You are the other who comes to me
If I open to another you're born in me
David Adam

Discussion and Action

1. Discuss the implication of David Adam's poem for Gonzague Pierre Louis, Claudino Ernest and many others like them.

2. What must our response be to the disabled people in our communities?

Reflection 2

Heavenly Almighty Father,
I am overwhelmed by the beauty of your presence.
As I sit on the beach near St Matthew's Church on Praslin,
I am filled with a sense of awe
at the sight of the white cross facing the sea.
I am discovering the more how deep is your love,
especially when the shallowness of my frail relationships
fades away in the intensity of your faithfulness.
There is so much that I still need to be unfolded to
because I cannot love as you love.
Through my selfishness I have deprived others;
my pride has oppressed those who sought you,
and my carelessness has brought despair around me.
How could I waste away the goodness you have entrusted to
    me?
How could I possibly have allowed death to cause destruction
    and damage?
How could I not have understood that you created me for a
    divine purpose?
Forgive me, Lord! I am a sinner in need of your attention.
The cross is here to remind me that nothing is impossible.
Love overcomes, for you are love.

Transform and renew me as I once again dedicate this life to
your service.
Jesus the Christ is alive – Hallelujah!
The Holy Spirit gives me the knowledge of his presence,
and with exultation I lift my voice and heart
to praise his holy name.
Glory, honour and power be yours for ever and ever!

Roger Chung Po Chuen, Mauritius

INDIAN KALEIDOSCOPE

Introduction

India has more than a billion people in a subcontinent which is as varied as it is extensive. It is a land of ever-changing pattern and colour, of diversity, excitement, uncertainty, mystery and great complication. It is a land of contrasts, of life and of death, of noise and dirt, and of light, music, dance and faith. There are the desperately poor, more than 312 million of them, living without enough food, clothing and shelter, and dying early; and there are the extremely rich, living in huge houses and even palaces. There are people from all the faiths of India who continue, following in the footsteps of the Mahatma Gandhi, Jawaharlal Nehru and others, to struggle to bring new life and freedom to the poorest of the poor.

Janet Stephens has written about her visit to Sevagram, one of the ashrams where Gandhi lived and worked.

> The focal point of the ashram is Gandhi's hut . . . it is a solid building constructed on a bamboo frame covered first with cow dung and then mud . . . The main room has simple palm tree mats spread on the floor, and a low wooden bench with a lantern on it. Here, at 4.45 am every day we joined the resident ashramites at morning prayer. . . . In the peaceful setting of the ashram I began to piece together all that Gandhi stood for. I learnt about his belief in cottage industry and the need he saw for villages to be self-reliant. The compact little spinning wheel, which opened and closed like a box, has become something of a symbol for manual labour, a means by which the very poor could earn their own bread and thereby regain dignity and self-respect.

Mrs Savithri Devanesen began her work for the village people of India almost by accident when she gave some of her jewels to a poor family so that they could put a roof on

Indian village scene
Jane Walton-Loxton

their house. She and her husband decided that what she had done was not enough and they began to organise for change over a large area. They planned for better healthcare and education, housing, employment and food for the village people. A huge network of projects has grown up, with good roads provided by the local government, day and night schools, care for cattle, and health centres for the people. The ordinary and the visionary are very close in India.

Quaker Glimpses of India

Chris and Christina Lawson

(Chris and Christina Lawson spent eight weeks of their sabbatical leave in India. They hoped to learn from a country and culture with which they were unfamiliar, and so to gain a fresh perspective on themselves and their own culture.)

The continuous encounter with a different culture provided fascination, frustration, warmth, discomfort and many other emotions. Riches and poverty we have seen before, but not in such close juxtaposition. The contrasts included affluent weddings and satellite TV, with a child begging while sweeping the floor of the train, and tile workers earning 50p a day.

We saw a society working hard to develop and modernise at a pace faster than the infrastructure can provide; overcrowded roads, inadequate water and sewerage systems, intermittent (though widely distributed) electricity supplies, schools and colleges full of those thirsting for education and coping with limited resources. Most schools seemed to be private, or run by churches, and so were fee-paying; free government schools were seen less often.

Here was an open-air society with innumerable trades and activities crowding the roadside; a labour-intensive and low-wage economy; no social security and minimal free health services.

We were likewise in a country where the majority religion, Hinduism, displayed practices and images with which we were often not familiar or comfortable. We also met aspects of Christianity with which we were uncomfortable and which we regretted. But we felt very close spiritually to some, both Hindus and Christians, whom we met.

We missed Quaker quiet, though we talked about it with Lutheran ministers, Catholic nuns, theological students and several sympathetic Hindus. We saw the Quaker approach to worship as a distinctive gift to share. A free style of worship was not unknown, particularly within the Pentecostal and Independent churches.

We sensed through visits, reading, and festivals in particular, the 4,000 years of history and culture that have produced India. We noted the great commitment to democracy of much of present-day India and the complexity of its politics with regional, religious, caste, party and economic interests all interwoven. With 16 states and a billion people, India felt well ahead of Europe in functioning as one unity, with many regional identities and autonomies.

Reflection

Savithri Devanesen gave her jewels to a poor family and this led her to a lifetime of work for the people of village India. Is sacrificial work of love for others often triggered by accident, a surprise to givers and receivers alike? Are accidents in this sense ever completely so?

Discussion and Action

1. What were the Lawsons' main impressions of India and how may they help us to understand this tantalising and challenging subcontinent?

2. Meet people from India who live in the UK. Listen to their stories, develop friendship.

Pluralism and Diversity

Caesar David

As I look around me
I find different cultures and different faces;
different creeds and different races.

And I wonder at
the conflicts which seem so natural and bound to be
in the diversity of people that surround me.

The debate turns into a war of forces –
which is better and which is worse?
who is a blessing and who is a curse?

What my mind refuses
is the alien fragrance, the wonder of another;
the differences in names of father and mother.

Lord, pardon my sin
of refusing to accept the beauty of your design
and to your gift of fullness let me thankfully resign.

Gracious God, grant
that I may learn to take and learn to give,
and in that sweet moment of sharing,
may learn to love and learn to live.

Dalits of India

There are about 250 million Dalits in India. They are those who are outside the caste system of Hinduism and therefore traditionally isolated and deprived. The word *Dalit* means oppressed people. 'Dal' comes from Sanskrit, meaning broken, torn asunder, trampled. Interestingly, in Hebrew 'dal' means low, weak, poor. Traditionally the Dalits do not draw water from a village well where caste Hindus live. They do not enter the village temple or eat in restaurants. Sometimes they are even expected to build their humble homes with a low entrance, so that they have to bend down every day as they go in and out. They do have constitutional rights, but for most of them this has made little practical difference. Christian Dalits are often found in separate churches. They do not receive the constitutional rights of other Dalits, simply because they are part of the Church.

P. Kambar has written about the Dalit people for a South Indian group.

India's Galileans

P. Kambar

One of the first names given to Christians during the first century was Galileans. It is important to know the role which Galilee plays in the Bible. The word *Galilee* literally means 'circle' or 'district' or region of Gentiles and foreigners.

The culture of Galilee was different from the culture in other parts of Palestine. Pharisees considered Galilean olive oil ritually impure. They also considered the men of Galilee as boorish, uncultivated and pugnacious. Galilee was considered an area where foreigners and polluted people lived. In this context, Deuteronomy 14:21 – forbidding the eating of animals which have died, and stating that these may be sold or given to aliens and foreigners to eat – comes to us as a shocking and, at the same time, somewhat familiar verse.

It is said that the Galileans condemned such laws, and refused to abide by the rules stated in the same chapter. In our country, dead animals in the villages are invariably given to Dalits for consumption and disposal. Such was the treatment extended to the Galileans. In Jesus' time, Galilee was the area where Jesus centred his ministry. This was the province where he ministered among such marginalised people at the risk of his life, and in the shadow of death.

His enemies branded him as Galilean (Matthew 26:69). They identified him with Galileans who at that time were considered unlettered conservative agrarians, but Jesus identified himself first with them, which led to the description of all the disciples as Galileans (Acts 1:11). No wonder Jesus earned the wrath of the Pharisees!

It is interesting to note that even after Christianity was well-established, the term *Galilee* was used in a kind of derogatory sense to refer to a porch or chapel at the west end of some churches, in which penitents were placed. It is important for us to remember that it is in the same region of Galilee that the risen Christ wanted to meet his doubting disciples. That is where the story of hope also continues.

Where do we have these Galilees today? In order to visit today's Galilee and to meet today's Galileans, one need not turn towards the west. These are right on our own doorstep, outside our compound walls, in the city, in the suburb and in the remote villages of India. They are the people who have been oppressed down the ages in the name of religion, in the name of purity, in the name of *status quo*. In other words, they are the Dalits in the context of India. They are the Galileans of today. Oppressed women also join their band.

Jesus was labelled Galilean. So were his disciples. Christians were called Galileans. The Church in India is full of Galileans. Should we not look at ourselves and examine what our attitude should be to all the issues which are challenging us today?

Reflection

How easily a religion may be used to marginalise and reduce the humanity of others.

Discussion and Action

Where are the Galileans in our society, those we are unwilling to touch or those generally pushed aside by religious or civic institutions? Go, meet and share.

Prayer Towards an Inclusive Community

Leela Rajanandam

Our loving Father and Mother,
    we have gathered together
    from different religions and life situations
    to meet each other,
    to understand each other's concepts
    and to build a genuine fellowship.

Our merciful God,
    enable us to understand our faith, ourselves, our society
    and to make us realise we are all one in the community.

Our loving God,
    we pray for all human beings who are in crisis, agitation,
    and the inequality of being male or female,
    rich and poor, upper and lower class.

Lord,
    please help us to change this structure
    and help us to realise what we have done.

Creator God,
    help us to acknowledge and respect each other
    as human beings in your image.

Lord,
    lead us out of anarchic society
    where human rights are violated,
    freedom curbed and survival doubtful.
Deliver us from all powers of subjection and dehumanisation,
    for all power is from your kingdom, power and glory.

Lord,
    please help us to recognise the need of a relationship
    of dialogue with people of other faiths and cultures,
    and to seek more co-operation on common concerns
    like justice, peace and social issues.
Help us to find ways of ministering to a pluralistic society.

O Lord,
    if we dominate over our neighbours
    with our power, wealth, and a false sense of supremacy,
    please forgive us and help us to change this attitude.

Lord,
    make us think of other people who are differently abled,
    oppressed and sick (especially with AIDS),
    and enable us to consider that they, too,
    are part of our community.

Lord, make us instruments
    of bringing people into one community.
Help us to become bridge-builders in solidarity
    to form a global community.

Faces of Women

The faces are as varied as India itself. There are the professionals and those with high social status. More women are educated and employed now and, like educated women everywhere in the world, they face greater expectations from their families and their country. Most women, however, like most people in India, are poor, rural, uneducated and exploited. The poor who work are in farming, in building, in trading and in domestic service. They work long hours, receive low pay and have no security. They make a greater contribution to society than men, but they face greater violence.

Malika is typical of many Calcutta sex workers. She was born into a family where her mother worked and her father was a cripple. Her parents both died when she was very young and she went to live with an aunt, where she was, at the age of around 12 years, raped by her uncle's brother. Malika panicked and ran away, struck up a friendship with a man who took her to Calcutta. Once in Calcutta the 'friend' took her to work as a prostitute.

Like Malika, many girls are tricked or forced into prostitution, where they begin a path to premature ageing and trauma. They are normally the breadwinners for their families. Some development groups are now focusing their attention on the children of the sex workers, offering them education and healthcare in the hope of breaking the cycle of deprivation for at least a few girls.

A Woman's Prayer

Rachel Mathew

O God, the giver of life,
    thank you for creating me as a woman
    by allowing me to share your image.
Thank you for the gift of life,
    the gift of my body, my womb,
    which enables me to participate in creating new life.
Thank you for the gift of your sacrificial love,
    which enables me to care and nurture
    children, aged, invalids and nature.
Thank you for breaking your body for all.
By sharing it, I'm strengthened
    when my body is broken and humiliated.
Lord, in the midst of suffering, oppression,
    discrimination and humiliation,
    you are my hope, my strength and my comfort,
    for you suffer with me and have conquered death.
Lord, help me to strive on to nurture life
    in the midst of my struggles against the powers of death.

The Sleeping Destitute.

Only in sleep can the destitute escape
from the world of reality which anchors him to
the pavement that is his pillow – western man
with a pillow of materialism and comfort
cannot evade the same reality, for which he
shares a responsibility

The Sleeping Destitute
Frances Meigh

Calcutta: City of Death and Life

Dorothy Clay's story is of a child living on Calcutta's Howrah Station who meets a group of visitors from England. Shourabh, the child in the story, represents the 100,000 children in Calcutta and the thousands in every big Indian city who live on the streets. They are alone, sometimes abandoned; they are almost always lost, vulnerable, hungry and lacking access to education or healthcare. Shourabh, a child labourer, epitomises some hope for the future.

The Railway Station

Dorothy Clay

My name is Shourabh and I live in Calcutta. I sleep and work at Howrah Station. It is the biggest and busiest station in India. I clean and polish the shoes of the people who pass through the station from all over the world. I particularly like to clean the shoes of the white people who come from countries a long way from India.

I first saw the party from England on a Thursday morning. In the crowded, noisy station, they put all their bags and cases and jackets in a big pile on the dirty forecourt. The Indian gentleman who was escorting them took their leader to the ticket office. They stood about in turn to protect their belongings. I banged my shoebrush on my box and pointed to the shoes, black lace-ups, which the only other man in the party was wearing. Yes, all the rest of the party were women, some of them beautiful young women with long fair hair and bare arms and jeans. Most of them wore boots, but I don't often get the chance to clean ladies' footwear.

The man in black shoes was reading a newspaper and

133

obviously had plenty of time to spare. So I was pleased when he nodded as I put my wooden step down in front of him. He put one foot on it, and I knew my three rupees were on the way. I made a good job of the polishing . . . they were not really too dirty before I started. The wearer of the black lace-ups took a wad of notes from his purse, consulted with his wife, and then asked me how much. I said three rupees, and he gave me a five-rupee note. He waved his hand which meant I could keep the change.

I watched two of the older ladies as they went into the coffee room and bought a sandwich and sweet coffee. As they came back on to the forecourt, I banged my stick on my box and grinned at them. They pretended not to notice me; a lot of them do that.

The younger ladies had been choosing magazines, some paperback books and some sweets for their journey. They still had time to spare as they waited for their escort to return with their tickets. They seemed to be rich enough to be travelling first class on reserved seats. None of that party would miss three rupees, even five rupees, for clean, shiny shoes for travelling out of Calcutta grime into the beautiful Indian countryside. How I wished the fair young woman with long fair hair, bare arms and tight jeans would let me clean and polish her footwear for her journey into the fresh air of the Indian countryside. She might even be going to visit our family's village.

Before I was born, my own dear mother came into Calcutta with my two big sisters and our father. Life was hard for her and she died soon after I was born in our shack at the roadside. My big sister looked after me for a few weeks, but then, when Father did not come back one night, an Indian lady in a long, white sari with pink edging – a friend of Mother Teresa, whom people call the Mother of India – said they would look after me and then find a family to care for me. My sisters were crying and wanted to go with the sister-lady as well, but she was only looking for babies that night. When she turned her back, my sisters ran away with me into the roadside shacks.

My big sister, Mun Mun, made friends with our auntie. My little sister and I soon learned to walk and to help Auntie and Mun Mun to scrape a living.

Auntie's brother used to clean shoes at the station. Before he left them to take a proper job on the railway, Auntie asked him to show me how to clean shoes. I was only seven years old but I was soon the champion polisher. People really are lucky to have me cleaning their shoes!

While I was daydreaming about where these English people might be travelling to, the men returned with the tickets. They all picked up their big bags and cases, grabbed their cans and bottles of water, paperbacks and chocolates, and trailed through the platform gate. It was the train for my mother's village! I just had to follow them. My fair lady was tying her bootlaces, so near to me that I banged my brush on my box, so quietly that only she heard me. I pointed to the boot she was tying – she smiled – and, as I put the box down, she put her boot on it and finished the knot. I rubbed on the polish, then brushed and brushed, and spat and spat, once for each side, brushed and brushed again, then rubbed and polished.

The carriage door in front of her opened and her friends pushed her through. What about the second boot? I followed her on to the train, and nearly lost her. When she found her reserved seat I placed the box beside her other foot. She was laughing, and her friends were laughing. Some of them took a photo. I always smile for that! My fair lady pressed a 10-rupee note into my hand as I picked up my brush and box and made a rush for the carriage door. As the train puffed out of Howrah Station, making for my own mother's village, I banged my brush on my box for joy, knowing that someone I loved was going to visit my own family's village. One day I shall travel on that train.

Tonight I shall take my fifteen rupees to my night school and I shall be able to buy my own exercise book and pencil so I can practise my letters and figures to become a real educated boy. The future of India depends upon children like me.

Photo: Gordon Couch

Howrah Railway Station in Calcutta

Reflection (from which discussion and action may follow)

We are guilty of many errors and many faults
but our worst crime is abandoning the children,
neglecting the fountain of life.

Many of the things we need can wait.
The child cannot.
Right now is the time his bones are being formed,
his blood is being made and his senses are being developed.
To him we cannot answer, 'Tomorrow.'
His name is 'Today'.

Gabriella Mistral

Kolata Stick Dancing
*Drawn, painted and printed
by the children of Sita School, Visham, Silvepura*

Jane Sahi's Life of Stories

I have visited the art ashram and school run by Jane and Jyoti Sahi twice and on both occasions I have been aware of entering a community of the ordinary people of the area, in a small village which was geographically close to the rapidly growing city of Bangalore, and yet, in terms of the transformation and uplifting of the spirit engendered by the journey, hundreds of miles away and in a different world.

In the ashram, and in the school run by Jane, an atmosphere has been created which makes it possible for the ordinary and usually materially poor people, and especially the children, to express themselves through painting, story and drama. One of my visits was on the occasion of fifty years of India's independence when the children in the school acted out the history of their country. Our entertainment was vivid, bright and very active. I returned to Bangalore deeply enriched and carrying with me one of the attractive and interesting calendars, of paintings and stories, created by the children.

My Work in Sita School

Jane Sahi

It is now nearly 30 years that my husband and I have lived on this same plot of land near a village about 30 kilometres from the city of Bangalore in South India. It was just a week before our eldest daughter was born that we bought an acre of land. The land was bare save for one solitary thorn tree.

Thirty years later much has changed and yet much has also continued. In the first few years our efforts to grow trees were largely thwarted by marauding goats. In addition, to water the trees required drawing water from an open well, bucket by bucket, with the aid of a pulley and rope. However, some of the trees from those early years have survived and now tower above the single-storied, red-brick, granite and tiled roof structures that make up our home, and work space. The garden is now full of flowering and fruiting trees.

The changes in the nearby village of Silvepura have been dramatic. In the course of thirty years we have seen the village change from being quite a remote, agricultural-based village to the beginning of a suburb to the city of Bangalore. Many have sold their land to developers or speculators and now work in the industrial estates that fringe the city. Previously there was no electricity, no medical service, no public transport, no tarred road and only an ill-attended primary school to serve the needs of the young.

The two nearest villages to our home are unusual, being made up entirely of Christian families. All the surrounding villages consist of Hindus and Muslims.

The Christian villages grew up in this particular area following a severe famine in the 1870s which had left in its wake many displaced orphans. The British government entrusted a group of orphans to the Paris Mission and allocated an amount of scrubland to be distributed for cultivation as the orphans reached maturity.

My husband Jyoti is an artist and comes from North India. His father was a Hindu and his mother was a Christian who had come from England as a teacher to work in one of the newly set-up 'national schools', run somewhat on Gandhian lines. His work has orientated to discovering a way of expressing his faith beyond the conventional images of a colonial past that continue to dominate the Church to the present time. He has sought to integrate his Christian faith with the rich Indian heritage of stories, symbols and images in a creative way.

My own work has focused on a small non-formal school. The school has been an effort to find a way of making learning more relevant and meaningful to some of the children in the nearby villages who, for various reasons, have not entered mainstream schooling.

The educational system in general is largely geared to serve the interests of the already privileged, and so the disadvantaged and first generation school-goers tend to get further marginalised. A recent survey revealed that one-third of all children in India between 6 and 14 years are out of school. (PROBE – Public Report on Basic Education, OUP, 1998)

Our home has also undergone considerable changes with five children growing up and an 'open house' that has meant a constant flow of visitors, some staying for years together. The people who have stayed for longer periods have generally been those interested in art or the school.

We have all inevitably been touched, changed and worried by the widespread repercussions of globalisation that have led to aggressive advertising and a growing consumerism. We have also been disturbed by the increasing tendency towards fundamentalism among many Christians and Hindus. Often we see a closedness, suspicion and rigidity by religions which had begun a flowering towards openness, dialogue and sharing.

Weaving in and out of our own life stories there have been a number of stories that give cohesion and hold together our searchings. These are stories that both 'hide and show what's hidden' and in subtle but powerful ways 'by indirection, have found direction out'. Stories have come upon us sometimes like the wayside shrines that a pilgrim passes which are stopping places for reflection and nourishment and provide signs for the uncertain way.

The children in the school come from Hindu, Muslim and Christian families. It has been an important element in the school to share each other's stories and festivals. A story often gives space for the child to make it his or her own in a way that moral maxims cannot. The children are encouraged to paint, draw, retell and sometimes dramatise the stories they hear. Jyoti in his work has explored both in writing and painting a wide range of stories, including tribal stories.

The story often speaks in a language of the imagination and heart. Joseph Campbell describes the folk tale as 'the primer of the picture language of the soul'. The story is both particular and universal and so crosses barriers of time, creed and nationality. The tale is continually reborn in different shapes and guises.

Idries Shah writes in his introduction to *World Tales*:

Perhaps above all the tale fulfils the function not of escape but of hope. The suspending of ordinary constraints helps people to reclaim optimism and to fuel the imagination with energy for the attainment of goals whether moral or material.

Stories cannot be hidden or stored in a niggardly way for they demand to be shared. There is a Kannada story that tells of a woman who refuses to share her story and song. The trapped story and song determine to take their revenge by taking the shape of a man's shoes and coat. When the husband returns home and spies the stranger's clothing, he doubts his wife's fidelity and demands an explanation. The wife is bewildered and her silence further enrages her husband. In great indignation he refuses to sleep in the house and so spends the night in a nearby temple. It is there that the husband learns the truth by overhearing a conversation between the lamp flames of the town that gather there to spend each night while the people sleep. The following morning he returns home and demands to be told the secret story and song. However, his wife has now no means to recall them. She has lost the gift that was given because of her inability to give it away.

Storytellers, however, cannot always find a listener. In another story an old woman searches far and wide to find an audience for her story. Everyone she approaches claims to be busy and tells her that they cannot spare the time to listen to mere tales. At last she persuades a salt-seller to pause in her work. The salt-seller herself becomes distracted but her unborn child listens attentively from within the womb. The knowledge the unborn child gains is to bring him wisdom and good fortune throughout his life.

One of the most common themes to many stories is the search for lost or sometimes unknown treasure. Such a search sometimes costs the protagonist not only his possessions and sense of security but his very life. Yet the quest is irresistible and brings its own fulfilment.

There is a Hottentot story related by Laurens van der Post that tells of a hunter who momentarily glimpses the reflection of a large, magical white bird. He forsakes everything familiar – family, friends, land and work – in an effort to see the marvellous bird again. But his search is in vain. Weary and despondent from his endless journeying, he comes at last to a mountain where it is rumoured the great bird lives. He begins the difficult climb but realises that he no longer has the strength to continue. In utter despair he lies down to await death and it is just at that moment of great emptiness that a white feather flutters from the sky. He grasps it with his dying hand and dies in peace. The story concludes that it was through this one man's travail and joy that his whole tribe found meaning and purpose to their lives.

The nature of treasure itself is often not recognised and it is sometimes only through an experience of loss that treasure becomes valued. There is a tribal story of central India called 'The Karam Tree'. In this story five brothers return from the city to their forest home, laden with precious goods from the market. Their journey has been long and tedious, but as they near their native village they eagerly anticipate a royal welcome.

The five brothers decide to rest a little distance from their village and to send one of their number in advance to announce their imminent arrival. However, as no one returns, one by one the brothers leave their purchases until only the eldest brother remains. The eldest brother, aggrieved and impatient, decides to go himself and find out the reason for this discourtesy. As he nears the village he is surprised to hear the clamour of drumbeats and song. When he arrives he is infuriated to find all engaged in a frenzied dance that spirals round the branch of a sacred Karam tree placed in the centre of the courtyard. In a rage he wrenches the branch from the ground and breaks it in seven parts and tosses them angrily on the dung heap.

The villagers recognise the enormity of his folly in breaking their sacred dance and rejecting their joy of abandonment in honouring the tree. They lament:

> In breaking the tree
> you have broken yourself,
> your roots are ripped,
> your fruits are torn.
> The seeds and the dance
> must die still born
> for now we are trapped
> in an inescapable curse.

The eldest brother, now grief-stricken, realises what his moment of anger will cost him:

> Today I will leave
> all that I thought I knew.
> For now I know only
> that I know nothing
> and love no one.
> I have lost balance
> and fallen a prey
> to greed and desire
> and to possess.

He sees that the things he has bought from the city with such pride have turned to stone.

And so begins a long journey to rediscover the tree and to

restore it to its rightful place. The journey is made more difficult because the whole of creation seems against him – the rivers have become poisonous, the fruits withered and the cows drained of all milk. At last he reaches an island where he finds the tree weeping.

In a modern retelling of the story the tree asks:

My people, what have I done to you?
How have I offended you ?
Answer me!

The voices of the people respond:

You remind us of our fragility
while we want to assert our power.
You remind us of God's gifts for all
but we want to privatise and possess.
You remind us of creation's extravagance
but we want to limit, bank and hoard.
You remind us of freedom
and we have forgotten the meaning.
You remind us of joy.
While we want only to be entertained
you remind us of sacrifice.
We don't want to die and endlessly give,
we want to live for ourselves.

It is at this point of awareness and repentance that the tree allows itself to be carried back to the village – and so restores harmony again, not only in the village but in creation itself.

Sometimes a story reveals the folly of imagining we can hold and possess treasure. There is a Chinese story that tells of a priest who collected jewels and spent his time guarding and gloating over them. One day he was persuaded to show them to a friend. The friend was suitably appreciative but startled the priest as he was leaving because he thanked him profusely for the gift of the jewels. The priest hastened to explain that he had no intention of giving him anything. The friend then gently explained that there was no difference in their pleasure of looking at the jewels except that the priest had the botheration and expense of looking after them while the friend could just enjoy them.

There is a tribal story from Bihar that also reveals the nature of true wealth and the tragedy that ensues when people mistake mere material possessions for treasure. The story tells how a clan of iron smelters are so intent on producing more and more iron that they work day and night. Complaints are lodged in heaven and the god Dharmes sends messengers in the shape of birds to try and encourage them to change their selfish ways and curb their greed. The iron smelters not only spurn the warnings but they mock the birds by blackening one, dividing the tail of another and stretching out of all proportion the neck of a third.

Finally Dharmes himself comes in the form of a leprous child. The child is rejected by all until an old woman reluctantly gives him shelter and in return he sifts and guards her store of grain. It soon becomes clear that the child is no ordinary child and that he unaccountably has magical powers, whereby he wins all games despite his apparent weakness.

Mysteriously the output of iron declines. Animal sacrifices prove ineffective, so a human sacrifice is decided upon. The iron smelters choose the sickly child as their victim. The child is fired in a kiln but when at last the heat dies down and the kiln is opened the smelters are amazed to see the child, now unblemished, emerge astride a golden horse.

The smelters imagine that they too will acquire such wealth if they but undergo the same treatment. Accordingly they ask their wives to firmly seal them in the kiln and fire them. After the screams and shouts subside there is a heavy silence and when the kiln is finally opened the unhappy wives find only charred bones.

Gradually, in the bitterness of their grief, the women come

to realise that their husbands' deaths and their own misery are caused by greed. The women become the spirits of the trees of the sacred grove and so serve as an eternal reminder of the folly of pride.

There are innumerable stories that tell of the ambiguities of the quest. Its success rarely rests on calculated ambition. There is a Kannada story that tells of a poor woman who, by chance, pierces the palm of her hand while applying cow dung to her doorstep. Her hand swells and no human treatment relieves her discomfort. However, unexpectedly a golden sparrow is born from the same swelling. It is the golden eggs laid in her house by the same sparrow that make her a rich woman. An envious neighbour discovers her secret and so deliberately pricks her hand. However, she is disappointed to find that not only does no sparrow fly from her wound but that the hand became so acutely infected that it has to be cut off.

It is often the story that gives shape to our deepest longings and the comfort that these are somehow supported by powers of goodness.

Maxim Gorky writes:

In tales people fly through the air on a magic carpet, walk in seven league boots, build castles overnight . . . tales opened up for me a new world where some free and all fearless power reigned and inspired in me a dream of a better life.

There is a Sufi story which tells of the rich, pleasure-seeking prince of Balleh, Ibrahim, who while hunting a deer is separated from his companions. Suddenly in the loneliness of the forest and the heat of the chase he hears a voice as though from the earth itself. Three times he hears the challenge: 'Ibrahim, I did not create you for this. Is this the best that you can do with your life?'

Ibrahim is shaken and he reins in his horse to a halt. He

sees a shepherd and, dismounting from the horse, he exchanges his costly clothes and jewels, his horse and his weapons for the man's coarse robe. Ibrahim leaves the palace and tells his friends that he will search the whole world if necessary to discover the reason why God created him, and so begins a lifetime of pilgrimage.

Rumi, in his retelling of the story, comments:

> The exchange was made, and Ibrahim set out on his new life. He made such an extraordinary effort to catch the deer but ended up being caught by God . . . God lives between a human being and the object of his desire.

Our fickleness and confusion are sometimes mirrored in a story, as in the Jataka Story which tells how the Lord Buddha appears as the wise lion who halts the stampede of panic-stricken animals. The animals, a prey to their own fear, are fleeing from disaster when they hear that the sky is falling down and the earth is opening up. The lion questions the animals until a shame-faced rabbit admits that he is the source of the rumour. He relates how while he was sleeping beneath a bilwa tree something fell beside him with a resounding thud. The lion gently carries him back to the scene of his dream and there together they find a fallen, crushed fruit!

We, like the first disciples, are confused, even confounded, by Jesus' most disarming question, 'What do you seek?' because 'the heart's desire' seems so elusive.

> What do you seek?
> Cornered by the glare
> of the question
> I struggle for movement,
> for a sound
> which does not feel itself
> false before it's begun,
> knowing – below the masking

tape of synthetic
action and inaction,
without the solace of
thought or word –
that there is an answer
formed by the step
towards the other.
Where, how, why do you live?
Where, how, why do I live?

Rumi cautions in a poem that the story is the beginning and not the end of wisdom.

But don't be satisfied with stories, how things have gone with others. Unfold your own myth, without complicated explanation.

Woodcut of a Dancing Christ – Healer,
Reconciler, and Destroyer of Evil
Jyoti Sahi

Jyoti Sahi

Jyoti Sahi, Jane's husband, is an artist who has worked to integrate his Christian faith with the rich Indian heritage from many faiths and traditions, of stories, symbols, and images.

One of the many Christian themes Jyoti has worked with for a long time is that of the dancing Christ.

Jyoti sees the celebrant at the Eucharist as a dancer, representing the Christ figure. He has meditated on the Eastern Easter Vigil ceremony when a cross of fire is made by cutting a cruciform trench in the ground outside a church, and by lighting a fire in it. Jyoti writes, '. . . it becomes a cross of fire branded upon the dark breast of the earth.'*

Jyoti has also been influenced by the Hindu image of the Nataraja, the Lord of the Dance. Nataraja is a special representation of the Lord Shiva dancing at the centre of a flaming circle, which symbolises the cosmos, which may itself destroy or liberate. Nataraja is treading demons down, his drum is creation, his hand is protection and his foot is destruction.

Jyoti sometimes paints Christ as a drum, a point of reconciliation. Sometimes Christ is a drummer.

Jyoti sees the dancing Christ, like Nataraja, as the dancer of death and of life. The dance is both a demonstration of love and a cleansing from sin. It is an expression of the God within and at the same time an offering to God.

All over the world, including in India, dance is being introduced into Christian worship.

* From *Stepping Stones* by Jyoti Sahi, published by the Asia Trading Organisation in 1986.

Reflection

Jane is living a rich life, in the simplest of places.

Discussion and Action

Jane writes, 'Weaving in and out of our own life stories there have been a number of stories that give cohesion and hold together our searchings.'

Share some of your own life stories.

Share one story which has been a 'wayside shrine' for you, inspiring and focusing your life.

'But don't be satisfied with stories, how things have gone with others. Unfold your own myth, without complicated explanation.' Rumi

Write a story or paint a picture which expresses your deepest longings.

A Christian Artist: Solomon Raj

I met Solomon Raj when he came to the UK to speak at a conference I had arranged. One story stands out for me from Solomon's visit. After the conference I had to go to London for a meeting, before returning to the office in Leicester. Solomon was apprehensive about the journey and asked if he could stay in the conference centre, to read and reflect, and I arranged this. When I returned, the centre director came to me and said that they had so enjoyed having Solomon to stay that they had decided not to charge any fee.

Solomon, as an Indian Christian, has struggled throughout his life with the expression of Christianity in Indian ways. Like a few other Christian Indian artists, Solomon does use Indian symbols and traditions, including the delineation of the eyes and hands to give comfort and blessing. He uses the lotus flower – borrowed from Hinduism and suggesting the movement from darkness to light and from death to life – a lot in his work, and has written about it here. Many of his batiks show Christ either seated in the lotus posture or amongst the lotus flowers.

Solomon has always been keen to create works of art with a social message, ever aware that he lives in a country in which the few are very rich and the majority very poor. Here is one of his poems, inspired by St Luke's Gospel.

> Hunger, cold, sickness and death
> are razing around.
> Children are dying,
> masses of people are starving.
> May we think of the hungry
> and the naked
> before we ask –
> What shall we eat,
> or what shall we drink?

Woodcut: Refugees
Solomon Raj

One of Solomon's most inspiring woodcuts was prompted by the war between Bangladesh and India in the early 1970s. Solomon lives in eastern India, and he saw the refugees from Bangladesh, on the borders and in India. He saw the suffering of the people and also saw the Christ, suffering with the refugees.

The woodcut shows a father and mother with a child, sitting with a water pot near to them. Christ, wearing a crown of thorns and with wounded hands, kneels behind them, and puts an arm around them, but they are unaware of him. Art, like music and drama, may raise awareness.

My Life and Work

Solomon Raj

Early Life

A picturesque part of the south-east coast of India, where the rivers join the mighty sea, was my birthplace. I was brought up in this dreamland as the son of a schoolteacher, and the simple rural life made deep impressions on my mind. I lived to the full, a simple village life with sailboats on the waterways, sand beaches, coconut palms and cows and calves grazing around. I guess I started thinking in 'pictures' before I learnt to speak in words. At school I paid more attention to making pictures in notebooks for my classmates and these have earned me many friends. When I could go around in the locality I went to spend my free time with a village screen painter and signwriter. I was asked to mix colours for him in clay pans. Thus, early in life I acquired a feeling for colours and squirrel-hair brushes.

Some Academic Work

I graduated with a teacher's university degree and started my career not as drawing master but as a science teacher. I got acquainted with other artists in the area, especially men related to an academy named after an accomplished water-colour artist, Sri Dameria Rama Rao, who was already dead. With the encouragement of these artists I passed some examinations which entitled me to certificates in drawing and painting. But I had never used these certificates to earn a drawing master's job.

As time passed by, I went to the theological college, was ordained into the Lutheran Church and held several posts, mostly student chaplaincy, communication education, and directing a Christian radio production centre. Around that time (1964), I was sent to Indiana University, USA, for a graduate programme in Communication Education. I was privileged to take two higher-level courses in graphics, and enjoyed the work as part of the requirement for an MSc in Education. This is about the only academic work I have done in fine arts, and that interest and experience in graphics stayed with me, as can be seen in my later work with wood-block prints, linocuts, etc. But I moved on to some watercolour work of childhood days and to batiks, wood sculpture and some metal casting. Today my batiks and woodblock prints are better known. As I worked as director of a Christian radio studio, I became more involved in fine arts as a member of a secular arts academy, and regularly participated in one-person shows and group shows, and more recognition came to my work. At one time the District Collector asked me to do a one-day arts seminar for the children of all schools in the city and he gave me help. Later I held an exhibition in the City Hall on the invitation of the Mayor and again the District Collector cut the ribbon. He mentioned the concern for the poor and the oppressed which came out very clearly in some of my art works. During this time as the director of the radio studio, I had written and produced some Bible dance dramas, 'Yakshaganas', in a typical classical dance form of the area. Now some of the better known of these plays are on video cassettes fortunately, whereas in 1973, when these dramas were played to packed audiences on the stage, it was new for a Christian story to be told in the dance and song art forms which are native to our culture.

In 1976, I was invited by the Selly Oak Colleges to teach in the Department of Cross-Cultural Communications. By then I already had put in 20 years of work in India as a communicator. Birmingham gave me an opportunity for a deeper involvement and study of the cultural aspects of art, especially the history and meaning of Christian art. At the University of Birmingham, where I worked for my PhD, my guide, Professor Hollenweger, was an artist himself in song, poetry and dance. I taught some courses with him in the area of art and faith. In my work with the Cross-Cultural Department of the Selly Oak Colleges, I was better known for visual arts and story. With one group of Namibian students we produced together a booklet with stories and artwork from the students themselves. I had my share of showing my artwork both in the colleges and also in a major exhibition at the university. Four years after I left Selly Oak in 1983, I was invited again as a William Patton Fellow, when I worked on my meditations and batiks to produce a book, *The Living Flame*. At this time I started my work on another series of coloured woodcuts – on the theme of liberation in Luke's Gospel.

While in Birmingham in 1980, and as a part of the 1,000-year jubilee of the advent of Christianity to Russia, I was happy to be initiated to icon painting and gilding. In 1986 I was invited as an artist-in-residence to some Lutheran Colleges in the USA. In all these places, while doing some teaching work, I was deeply involved in art exhibitions, study of art and visits to various galleries and private art studios. My wife was with me in all these travels and she kept herself busy making beautiful tapestries.

More Extended Ministry

In 1986, my work as a church employee came to an end when I was officially made 'retired'. I continued my artistic activities more intensively. While doing art productions in my home town, I have travelled to several countries as artist-in-residence. In Japan I was guest of the Asian Christian Arts Association and I was introduced to Japanese woodblock printing which is a special technique. I am a life member of the Asian Christian Arts Association.

As soon as I had returned from the USA in 1986, I was elected as the President of the Indian Christian Arts Association in which special capacity I served the cause of Indian Christian art for five years. As President I was instrumental in two of the All-India Art Conferences, one in Bombay and another in Bangalore. At a meeting for the Asian Christian Arts Association in Bali in 1998 I presented a lecture on Indian Dances and Christian Faith. In this period I presented papers on art and culture and other related topics in many places, including India.

Another Face of Artistic Creativity

My involvement in another form of Indian art with strong cultural tones is Gospel Dance Drama (Yakshagana). Kuchipudi is a small town well known for a certain form of Indian dance drama. Kuchipudi dancers have told the stories of Hindu gods for more than 300 years. Christians in India have never touched the dance form since they learnt from some missionaries that dance is sinful and Hindu dances are idolatry. But when I came to radio work and got involved in indigenous song forms for broadcasting, I wrote and produced a major dance drama in Kuchipudi style, closely following the formal structure but putting in the Gospel content. Some Hindu dance experts and people trained in classical music have helped me in the effort and there was available documented reading material of a high academic standard on the subject. The title of my first Gospel Yakshagana was 'Kim Karthavyam', in Sanskrit meaning 'What is my duty?' The answer, of course, is 'Love God with all your heart and love your fellow human beings as yourself'. Taking trained Hindu girls as dancers and a well-trained orchestra, we gave the first performance in 1973 to a packed audience in our city and the response was most wonderful. Hindus who were knowledgeable in this art form were surprised that Christians would ever use such a form for communicating Bible stories. And they were happy that the medium was so successfully adopted. Immediately there were invitations from several places for our group to perform, and we accepted the calls taking all the dancers, singers and the orchestra to many places. The soundtrack was broadcast over the national radio, and the response was spontaneous and positive.

The response from Christians to these experiments was discouraging. First of all, many of my own church people did not think that Indian dance was 'holy' enough to convey the Gospel message. Dances were associated with temple women and some of the Church people thought that my dancers were not baptised Christian girls and so they should not tell the Gospel story. And finally also the beautiful body forms of these dancers and the traditional costumes and the ornaments offended some of the conservative church people, and we had great problems in the early days when we had expected appreciation and approval from the Christian audience.

But fortunately today there is less objection although there are not many Christian girls who learn the South Indian dance forms to tell the Gospel story. The great Christian master of Indian dances, a very accomplished performer and Catholic priest, Fr Barbosa, has broken the walls of prejudice, and there are a few excellent schools in India today experimenting with liturgical and pedagogical Indian dances.

Why Christian Art?

I have learnt from childhood that word and image go together. Pictures spoke to us in school more interestingly than the spoken word and printed page. As I grew up and tried to understand my faith, I have a little better understanding of the incarnational aspect of the word, more specifically the multi-cultural approach to the Gospel message. Now I am even more convinced that my faith should be better experienced and shared with others with the help of an art form, whether it is pictures or song dance or drama. Sometimes I ask myself the question, What makes art Christian? Or is there such a thing as 'Christian art'? Why do the non-Christian artists in India sometimes hesitate to accept me as an 'artist', seeing the subject matter of my pictures is mostly biblical. On the other hand, why do some Christians ask me whether I could convert anyone to Christianity through the use of my pictures.

I believe that a piece of art is not Christian because a Christian artist made it. A Christian subject is also not always necessary to make a piece of art Christian. So I would prefer to use an expression such as 'prophetic art' – art with a message, a piece of art which awakens the viewers and encourages them to ask questions, something which is open enough for the viewer to respond to and enjoy at a deeper level. Visual symbols have helped me a great deal in this process as they have helped many other artists through the ages. Symbols speak more deeply. Symbols many times are open in the sense that the viewer could, to some extent, give his or her own meaning, and then of course the viewer asks questions and learns from others and this enables a widening of perceptions.

A lotus, for example, is an Indian symbol which can speak to people at different levels. It could suggest simply beauty or purity, or it could be associated with gods and goddesses as their abode or seat or pedestal, or it may, to those who know it, suggest the old prayer of the Hindu scriptures: 'Lord, lead me from darkness into light, from untruth into truth and from death into life.' And going along a little further, to me, a Christian and an Indian, the lotus suggests the resurrection of Christ and of the believer.

This kind of adaptation of the message of a symbol has been done all along in the Christian Church. The Eastern Orthodox icon painters have borrowed a symbol like the nimbus (circle around the heads of divine persons), we are not sure from where, perhaps from the Roman emperor's portraits or from the Buddhist wall paintings of Ajanta and Ellora in India. But the symbolism is clear. It suggests glory, holiness and divine virtue. One Hasthamudra (hand gesture) of the Greek icons is very meaningful. Christ always holds his right hand up in a blessing gesture with the thumb and index finger joined together to make a circle. Scholars tell us that this is a visual statement of the doctrine of the two natures of Christ, divine and human, both conjoined and without confusion. Of course, we know that this doctrine is as old as the fourth century when the church answered questions on the Christological controversy.

So today when we want to speak to our Indian neighbours we have made the mistake of using Western imagery and symbols all the time and therefore seeming strange and unintelligible. As men like D. T. Niles have said long ago, we have received the sapling of the Gospel in a western pot and we did not allow the sapling to grow in the native soil. We have not even broken the pot.

So now we the Indian artists and Indian songwriters like to use Indian symbols like the lotus to give new meaning to the symbols. Many symbols adapt themselves to such a process. The red robe, the 'Padmasana' posture of the teaching Lord, the upheld Abhayahosta (comforting hand), the downturned left hand in Datha hastha (the gifting gesture), and many Indian symbols appear now in our art works. My artist colleague Jyoti Sahi made good use of the tree symbols. Recently I made a batik, using a symbol for the universal church and the famous 'Upanishadic' Aswatha tree with roots in heaven and branches

Batik: The Chariot Wheels of God
Solomon Raj

bearing fruit on the earth. How could I think of the kingdom of God better than in the imagery of a tree rooted in heaven and bearing fruit here on earth? There is a whole sermon there. Much more can be said about the symbols in the process of inculturation of the Gospel. Talking about the performing arts and the cultural idiom which I have used, scholarly Hindus went on record to say, 'We have never heard the Bible story in such an idiom (and with a such well-known flavour) as we see today.' For example, it is not easy to interpret the many contrasts in the prayer of St Francis of Assisi for peace in hand gestures and rhythmic steps, and when once we tried to do it people said that this speaks to their hearts even better.

Some people think that art should be for art's sake. But I think that art should have a message to contemporary society, to the issues confronting people.

The inspiration for me to do the Batik 'The Chariot Wheels of God' has come from an atheist Hindu poet in my country whose revolutionary songs questioning the unjust society and its structures had moved our hearts as youngsters in the 1940s. In this woodcut I tried to suggest God's presence by showing a hand projecting out of the clouds in the sky. This is the way some Christian artists have symbolically shown God's presence. In this picture there are light rays also, radiating from the hand. On the right side I show a man stepping forward with an anchor on his shoulder and with his right hand stretched out as a gesture of reaching God, of responding to his call. An anchor in Christian art has always suggested hope, as the ship suggested the Church. The waves under the man's feet symbolise the ocean, the sea of life, suggesting danger, sorrow and death.

Reflection

Like a bird in flight
I soar into the heights
seeking to reach
his peaceful realms.
Higher than the earth
and higher than the mountains
I go darting through
the cool, calm winds,
leaving behind me
the loads and cares of this life.
Solomon Raj

Discussion and Action

1. How would you define Christian art? Give some examples.

2. Look at a picture or pictures which inspire you and go on to write a song, story, poem or meditation. Alternatively make a group painting or collage.

3. Write and share a service of worship when you offer the new creations to God.

4. Identify a piece of art which encourages you towards social action.

A SPIRITUAL JOURNEY

Introduction

I have written to Nadir many, many times, but I have only met him once, and that meeting was enough for me to ask him to tell me more about his life journey and about his movement into Christianity from a Zoroastrian childhood and young adulthood. His own family remains Zoroastrian and he constantly pays tribute to them in his writing and in conversation with his friends.

In his story, which follows, Nadir includes the time when Bishop Christopher Robinson of the Delhi Brotherhood helped him to see that his vocation was loving and giving; in other words, opening himself to the sufferings of the world. Nadir has done this throughout his life, in his own work and in supporting and encouraging many other people and groups, including those who work through Christians Aware. He has been outstanding in his support of the poor and downtrodden of the world, and of those who work for racial justice and inter-faith understanding. He is someone who says the Magnificat every night.

Nadir has had a number of commonplace books published which give great pleasure and at the same time offer a remarkable resource.

A Spiritual Journey
Nadir Dinshaw

I must be one of the few members of Christians Aware not to have been born a Christian. I was in fact born a Parsi in Karachi, in what is now Pakistan but was then undivided India, in 1925.

Since this is an account of my spiritual journey I hope I may be forgiven if I elaborate a bit on the religion and the land of my birth, both of which have been of great importance to me on that journey.

Zoroastrianism, the religion of the Parsis, is numerically the smallest of the world's great faiths – our numbers do not exceed 150,000 in the whole world – and it is also the oldest of the monotheistic religions. In the words of Dr Mary Boyce, Professor Emeritus of Iranian Studies at the University of London, 'Zoroastrianism has probably had more influence on mankind, directly and indirectly, than any other single faith.' It was the state religion of three great Persian Empires, dominating the Near and Middle East for over a thousand years, and, from that vantage point of power and wealth, its influence and its doctrines successively permeated Judaism, Christianity and Islam.

Professor Boyce goes on to say that 'It was with humanity itself that Zoroaster's moral theology was most profoundly concerned' and 'the obligations to care for God's special creation, man, means that an individual should always be concerned for his fellows, and never simply self-regarding.'

Even Herodotus, at the dawn of the world's recorded history, did not fail to notice that for the 'Zoroastrian to pray for himself alone is not lawful, rather he prays that it may be well with the king and all Persians, for he reckons himself among them.' This accords well with the Zoroastrian practice to this day, for a Zoroastrian never prays for self alone, but for the whole community.

Zoroastrianism's cardinal tenets are simple – God is to be served by each individual practising the virtues of good thoughts, good words and good deeds, with a heavy accent being placed on good deeds – a Zoroastrian prayer goes so far as to say that good words and good thoughts are of little use unless they are swiftly followed by good deeds. Philanthropy is not therefore a pleasant optional virtue – it is basic to the faith. It is little wonder then that Bishop Gore

(1853-1932) referred to Zoroastrianism as 'the religion of the good life'.

How well Zoroaster's doctrine shaped the conduct of his followers, and how they in turn shaped the course of history, is, however, most evident in the conduct of the most powerful emperors Persia has ever produced, namely Cyrus and Darius. It was King Cyrus who freed the Jews from the Babylonian captivity in 539 BCE. He made no attempt to impose his Zoroastrian religion on his subjects, but his inscriptions bear live testimony to the fact that he encouraged each of his subjects to live a good life according to their own tenets. He allowed the Jews to rebuild their temple in Jerusalem, and Mary Boyce observes in this regard: 'This was only one of many liberal acts recorded of Cyrus, but it was of particular moment for the religious history of mankind; for the Jews entertained warm feelings thereafter for the Persians, and this made them more receptive to Zoroastrian influence.'

The Jews regarded Cyrus as one who was an agent of Yahweh. In the Old Testament, 2 Chronicles 36:22-23 reads: 'In the first year of Cyrus, King of Persia, in order to fulfil the word of the Lord spoken by Jeremiah, the Lord moved the heart of Cyrus, King of Persia, to make a proclamation throughout his realm and to put it in writing. This is what Cyrus, King of Persia, says: "The Lord, the God of Heaven, has appointed me to build a temple for him at Jerusalem."'

The first verses in the book of Ezra repeat this theme, and add that King Cyrus returned to the Jews 5,400 articles of gold and silver which the Babylonians had taken away from their temple in Jerusalem.

After the Arab conquest of Persia in the seventh century, those Zoroastrians who refused to convert to Islam fled to India, bringing with them their sacred fire; they were given sanctuary by the Hindu ruler of Gujarat, and it was there that they laid down their roots, and were given the name, Parsis, as being from Pars, the Greek name for Persia.

In their scriptures the Zoroastrians found references to a future Saviour, the 'Soshyant'. This wasn't Zoroaster himself but a Messiah who, coming from Ahura Mazda (God), would defeat the Devil and all his evil works for all time. The Zoroastrian sages (the Magi) had believed this for years, and, being astronomers, had searched the heavens with diligence until they saw the star and made their celebrated journey to Bethlehem. So the Feast of the Epiphany is one that has always had a great attraction for me, and this was deepened many years ago, when I first read Henry van Dyke's beautiful *Story of the Other Wise Man* which contains a lovely free translation of one of the hymns of the Gathas (the Zoroastrian scriptures).

Why then, you may well ask, did I choose to change my faith when I was in a religion which was undoubtedly inspired by God, whose precepts I admired greatly, and which was the religion of the person I loved most deeply – my grandmother. The answer may sound surprising.

From my childhood I had adored my grandmother – the most gentle, loving person I have ever known. She was a saint, and the very reverse of the sullen saints, from whom St Teresa so rightly asked to be delivered. My own brother, who also adored our grandmother, said to me once, many years after her death, that he could not imagine what sins she could possibly have committed, and when I read that it had been said of Bishop King, the saintly Bishop of Lincoln, that his was a face that God intended all humanity to have, I knew exactly what that meant.

Indeed, she carried her propensity for giving away all her possessions to such an extent that to prevent this her children had to lock her cupboard and keep the key themselves. Nevertheless, even this could not daunt my ever-generous grandmother; when a poor woman came to the house and asked my grandmother for a sari, my grandmother, knowing that she couldn't get hold of one, was overjoyed to hear the poor woman saying that she liked the sari my grandmother was wearing. To my grandmother this presented not one but two unassailable reasons for taking it off there and then and giving it to her: (a) the poor woman needed a sari, and (b) she liked the sari my grandmother was wearing very much. To my grandmother the first was ample reason for giving it – the second was a wonderful bonus – and she met my mother's remonstrances silently, but with an even more than usually angelic smile on her lovely face, completely convinced of the rightness of her action.

So in my eyes, then and now, my grandmother was as near perfection as it was possible for a human being to be, but the figure of Our Lord in his Divinity and of Our Lady in her divine humanity showed an even greater degree of perfection – in his case an absolute perfection. My grandmother, in her near perfection, was an exemplar of love and beauty, only to be surpassed by the one perfect sinless Being and his Mother, who in her simplicity was favoured by God, and was to be called blessed by all generations. I must, I felt, without losing one iota of all the beauty of my Zoroastrianism faith, take it with me into my Christian one.

There are two modern prayers by different Persian Christians that I say regularly, and which are a source of joy and comfort to me. The first says:

Lord Jesus Christ, at your birth
    your ever blessed Mother received on your behalf
    from my ancestors the Magi
    the most valuable gifts they had;
    grant, I beseech of you,
    that I, a Persian of the twentieth century,
    may also, by her holy intercessions,
    find the humble offering of all that I have,
    and all that I am,
    equally received by you,
    now and for all the days of my life.
Amen.

The second one is similar:

> Almighty God,
>> who when you sent your blessed Son Jesus Christ
>> into the world for our salvation,
>> didst give to our ancestors the Magi
>> the grace and honour of admittance to his presence,
>> grant that we, Persians of the twenty-first century,
>> may also, like them, be granted the same grace,
>> thus entering into the fuller inheritance of our
>>> forefathers,
>> to the glory of your Holy Name.
>
> Amen.

The main gifts of that inheritance of spiritual beauty were for me a passionate concern for the poor and the oppressed, and especially for the victims of discrimination, and an equally passionate concern for what one of my greatest heroes, Archbishop Trevor Huddleston, called inter-faith ecumenism, together with an abhorrence of religious fundamentalism of any kind.

I suppose it would have been comparatively easy for me to have become a 'brown Englishman' or an 'honorary white' – I have often been the recipient of the 'Oh, but we don't mean you' syndrome when I have been talking about race, and I have always rejected it very firmly. To accept such a description was never an option for me. When I was a small boy at my public school in England, I remember walking up the Hill at Harrow where a plaque set in the wall of the Old School recorded that it was at this point that Anthony Ashley-Cooper, afterwards 7th Earl of Shaftesbury, had seen a pauper's funeral, which made him dedicate his life to the service of the poor. I remember, very clearly, also making a vow that when I grew up I too would do all I could for the poor and the underdog.

Many years later Archbishop Joost de Blank, whom I loved

very dearly, said to me, 'Remember you have privileges denied to most of your coloured brethren; use them always for their benefit; defend them against the powerful; and always be a voice for the voiceless and the oppressed.'

Above all, from my childhood, perhaps because India is so pre-eminently the land of the mother, and because, as I have said before, the greatest influence in my own life has been my adored grandmother (my mother's mother), I have always had a deep devotion to Our Lady, the Anawim, the Mother of the poor and their protectress.

When Dorothy Day, the great American radical and saint, the founder of the Catholic Worker movement, was asked how she could do the things she did – marching, protesting, breaking the law, going to jail – her invariable answer was 'I am a daughter of the Church.' I am not worthy to touch the ground Dorothy Day walked on, but when I am challenged on the things that I say about race or poverty, when I am upbraided for being harsh, I also have a one sentence reply: 'I am a child of Our Lady of the Magnificat.' I say the Magnificat every night with deep penitence, for I am always aware of how far I fall short of it, but I am always equally aware that in it Our Lady shows forth the will and ways of God, and the nature of his kingdom – the mighty put down, the humble and the meek exalted – and that it cannot, and must not, be spiritualised away.

It was not, however, until I was in my middle 30s that I actually became a Christian. I had wanted to be one from my adolescence, but what kept me from taking this step was my deep distaste for Christian exclusivism; how could I, surrounded as I had been from my childhood by the most lovely examples of lives of holiness among people who were not Christian, believe that all these people were *per se* inferior to Christians, leave alone that they were in themselves not just inferior but condemned, because they were not baptised Christians, and in fact adherents of another great faith? I had no desire whatever to belong to such a faith – my attitude was the same as that of Queen Elizabeth I, when she said to the Spanish Ambassador, rejecting his claims about the fate of those who were outside the Roman Catholic Church, 'And what is it to Your Grace if my subjects go to Hell in their own way?'

Fortunately, I had read enough to realise that there was a Christian inclusivism, which, whilst by no means ideal, did permit me to belong to the Church with a tolerably clear conscience.

Then, in 1959, I joined the Samaritans in London, having read an article about the organisation in a Church paper, something that has been a great influence in my life. Although the founder, Prebendary Chad Varah, was an Anglican priest, and we were located in a City church, St Stephen Walbrook, where he was Rector, the whole ethos, under his compassionate and brilliant leadership, was one of total acceptance in every way, regardless of class, creed or sexual orientation. Indeed religious, or any kind of, indoctrination was banned – the only criterion was the wellbeing of the client. I owe an eternal debt of gratitude to Chad for creating an organisation where we all met and worked together, and were friends together, regardless of our faith or lack of it; as a very new convert to Christianity, who still clung tenaciously to the validity of my own faith, this was a great comfort. As Chad frequently reminded us, the Samaritan did not say to the man who fell among thieves, 'I cannot look after you, because you worship and believe differently to me'; yet it was he, the outcast Samaritan, whom our Lord chose to be the inheritor of eternal life. How I wish and pray that all Christian exclusivists today would accept this truth, so that the Church might be seen as having some relevance to the world outside its walls.

Even in the nineteenth century two great souls from different faiths – Swami Vivekananda and Mr Gladstone – had much in common, for Swami Vivekananda said, 'I do not understand how people declare themselves to be believers in God, and at the same time think that God has handed over to a little body of men all truth, and that they are guardians of the rest of humanity'; and, in an equally noble passage, Mr Gladstone, high churchman though he was, could say, 'I do not believe that God's mercies are restricted to a small portion of the human family . . . I was myself brought up . . . to believe that salvation depended absolutely upon the reception of a particular and very narrow creed. But long, long, have I cast those weeds behind me.'

And I count it as one of the privileges of my life that I enjoyed the friendship of Marjorie Sykes, Quaker, Gandhian, author, friend of Gandhi and Tagore, friend and biographer of C. F. Andrews, and one of the greatest Western figures in Indian life, who died a citizen of India. In a typically lovely passage, she says, 'We all know the fruits of the Spirit and recognise the beauty of holiness in our own ancestral tree. . . . The flowers of unselfish living may be found growing in other men's gardens and rich fruits of the Spirit may be tasted from other men's trees. The kingdom of the new birth, the kingdom of God, transcends our human boundary lines.'

And there are two stories from India which are jewelled cameos of those rich fruits of the Spirit of which Marjorie spoke.

Andrew Harvey, the brilliant writer, tells in his book *A Journey in Ladakh* of an incident told to him by a friend of his.

I was in Pokhara once, sitting in a coffee house by the lake. It was cold. There was a beggar woman, very old and thin, sitting on the wooden benches outside, who asked me for some money. I gave her five rupees. She bought herself a meal, a soup of vegetables and potatoes. Then she did something extraordinary. There was a particularly mangy, filthy mongrel skulking about the door of the coffee house. The woman sat down on the ground with the dog, and gave it exactly half her food. They ate together. She had nothing, no money, hardly any clothes; the dog was not hers. I did not feel she had said to herself, 'I am going to share half my food with the dog.' No, she gave her food simply, spontaneously, without any sense, I saw, that she and the dog were different; or yet that there was any obligation on her part to give, or on its part to be grateful. That is compassion.

The other story was told to me recently by a Sacred Heart sister who lived for a time in an ashram in Rishikesh, a most sacred place to Hindus, as being the source of the River Ganges. Every day she used to walk to the river to say her prayers. One day the hem of her skirt got torn, and she took it to the poor Hindu tailor whose sole assets were his sewing machine and the little wooden cabin in which he sat cross-legged all day earning his tiny pittance. When she went to collect it the next day, she asked how much she owed. 'Nothing,' he replied. 'Nothing?' she asked, surprised. 'Nothing,' he repeated. 'But why?' she asked, and he replied, 'Every day I see you going to the river to say your prayers. You are not a tourist, this means you are a seeker – how can I take money from a seeker?'

Over and over again in India you will see examples of what I can only call the divine humanity, and it exists frequently between practising members of different faiths, for to the Eastern mind the saying from the Vedas – 'Truth is one, sages call it by different names' – is a widely accepted fact, not a contentious proposition. Fr Bede Griffiths, the Benedictine monk who lived for 40 years in an Indian ashram, declared in some memorable words, 'I have to be a Hindu, a Muslim, a Parsi, a Jain, a Sikh, a Jew, if I am to know the truth, and to find the point of reconciliation in all religions' – an alien concept to the Western mind, but an obvious truth to an Eastern one.

It was in the 1960s, in Bombay, that I was privileged to meet, and to learn from, Christians of deep spirituality and wide open hearts – the Cowley Fathers, and the Wantage Sisters, Bishop William Lash, the Anglican Bishop of Bombay, and very soon the Metropolitan of the Church of India, Pakistan, Burma and Ceylon, and Bishop Christopher Robinson who succeeded Bishop Lash – what I owe to them is something I can never repay, and I have golden memories for which I am deeply grateful.

The Cowley Fathers were responsible for a school for largely destitute children, of very underprivileged backgrounds; some were the children of prostitutes, some were orphans, or abandoned by their parents, all were poor.

I shall never forget a confirmation I attended there. Bishop Lash, as befitted a Franciscan, was not renowned for sartorial elegance (when I first met him I only realised he was the Bishop by the small wooden cross he wore), yet, for this confirmation, he was resplendent in what was obviously his best cope and mitre. The infinite gentleness and tenderness with which he confirmed each child, by name, was something I still remember with wonder and gratitude, after nearly 40 years. The beautiful chapel was ablaze with lights, and I realised that whatever the future of these children might be, into whatever sad paths life might lead them, whenever they found themselves abandoned or exploited they could at least have what Dostoevsky called 'this one good memory' upon which to draw.

The Metropolitan of the Church of India, Pakistan, Burma and Ceylon at that time was the charming, Oxford-educated, Cuddesdon-trained Dr Lakdasa de Mel – an urbane, witty, and brilliant mimic and raconteur, whose family had ruled in Ceylon in the sixteenth century. Yet he once held a group of Samaritans in the vestry at St Stephen's spellbound for 20 minutes when he told us of a visit he had made, with the Bishop of Assam, to the bedside of a poor, young, dying woman who, as her last action on earth, had given him her sole wealth – five rupees and a pair of tiny gold hoops, with the words 'for Jerusalem'. His eyes were brimming over with tears as he told us this. Significantly his last action on his own deathbed was to sign the transfer of the last piece of his own property to the Sri Lankan Samaritans.

It was Fr Wain of the Cowley Fathers, a gentle sensitive saint, who, knowing of my unhappiness about Christian exclusivism, sent me a wonderful piece of Christian pluralism by that marvellous seventeenth-century Christian divine, William Law, which began, 'There is but one salvation for the whole of mankind and that is the life of God in the soul. . . . Now there is but one possible way for man to attain his salvation, or Life of God in the soul. There is not one for the Jew, another for the Christian and a third for the Heathen. No, God is one, human nature is one, salvation is one and the way to it is one and that is the desire, for the soul turned to God.'

Christopher Robinson, who succeeded Bishop Lash as Bishop of Bombay, was the person who had the greatest influence on my spiritual life. He embodied Christianity, and not just Christianity, but spirituality at its most attractive; and he was blessed with the looks of a Bishop King. Olivier Clement once wrote of the 'theology of faces', and after my grandmother, Bishop Christopher was the best exemplar of that theology. I remember reading in some journal the words of an Anglican priest who said, 'No Anglo-Catholic can deny without blasphemy the God-given graces, truths and beauty of the other great religions', and when I told Bishop Christopher this, he smiled his wonderfully gentle smile, and said, 'Oh! But Nadir, I've known that all my life.'

That wonderfully gentle smile vanished when I gave him a book on humility by a well-known Christian author, which began, 'Humility is a specifically Christian virtue'; he bounded out of his chair, walked on to the verandah outside his study, from where we could see the stream of manual labourers going home after an arduous day's work, the women with their babies on their backs. 'Do you see all these dear people, Nadir; how many of them do you think are Christians?' he asked me. 'Very few, I should imagine,' I said. 'Yes,' he replied, 'and yet look at them in their poverty and in the grace and dignity they have – that is humility, and acceptance, Nadir'; and then he said something that I have never forgotten. 'Remember, Nadir, there is no such thing as a specifically Christian virtue; all the great virtues are universal; and *no* faith can claim a monopoly of them; there are Christ-like virtues,' he went on, 'but those are usually to be found more often in non-Christians than in Christians – never forget this, Nadir, never, never.'

I have so many memories of my beloved Bishop Christopher. One I particularly cherish is the sight of him and a Hindu 'sannyasi', neither of whom knew the language of the other, feeding each other alternately with the flakes of a single orange, then looking at each other for about ten minutes with great love in their eyes, till they both got up, made a deep 'namaste' to each other, and then, two men of God, they parted. I felt as if I had been on a different planet.

It was in Bombay, too, that I first experienced one of the two great landmarks of my journey. It was, and is, a deeply personal experience, and I hadn't at first wanted to mention it here, but John Austin, one of my closest friends, insisted that I should.

Bishop Christopher was in a very real sense my 'guru'. I was deeply dissatisfied with myself – with my lack of any business or practical ability, of any appreciation or knowledge of music or the arts, and with what felt like a rather arid and unsatisfactory spiritual life. We were talking about this one day, and he listened quietly to what I was saying, and then said, 'Nadir, what do you like doing? What do you think you can do? Do think about it over the next few days, and we'll talk about it next week.' So I went away and thought about it, and the only things I could try to do were to be loving and giving, and that sounded so vague and inadequate. Anyway I went back after a few days and Bishop Christopher asked me what I thought I could do. I muttered something about loving and giving, and saw Bishop Christopher smile and nod his head in agreement, as if he had known all along, as indeed it transpired he had; for he said to me, 'I knew you had a vocation to be loving and giving, but I wanted you to see it for yourself. But, Nadir, loving and giving doesn't mean just being kind to elderly bishops – it means opening yourself to the sufferings of the world, it means standing with Our Lady at the foot of the Cross; if you can do that, then come into my Chapel, and I will give you my love, my prayers and my blessing.' Thirty-five years later, when I was again feeling particularly useless, Bishop Richard Holloway, another of my closest friends, wrote to me that he considered that I had a vocation 'to stand with the Holy Mother at the foot of the Cross your station keeping'. Never have words affected me more deeply; after a gap of 35 years I was transported back to that little chapel in Bombay, with my beloved Bishop Christopher's words still ringing in my ears.

The second significant and transforming experience of my spiritual journey was also concerned with Our Lady, and the vital part she has played in my life.

I have already mentioned the Sacred Heart sister and the tailor at Rishikesh. The ashram where she lived was founded by, and has as its Acharya (or head), another Sacred Heart sister who is one of the greatest spiritual figures in India. Like me, Mataji (or Reverend Mother) Vandana was born a Parsi, but there the resemblance ends. After teaching for some years in Bombay, she felt called to immerse herself more and more in Indian spirituality, and lived in Hindu ashrams before founding her own, where she conducts Hindu/Christian retreats, inter-faith dialogue and worship, and various other activities that would be deeply offensive to many Christians! She also writes books in which there is a constant interplay of Hindu and Christian spiritual thought. For instance, she will draw out similarities between Mother Ganges and Our Lady which are both original and beautiful, and in one of her books, *And the Mother of Jesus Was There*, dedicated to Our Lady, she said, 'I lay it at the feet of my Gurudev Sri Swami Chidananda who taught me to sing, "Om Maria Rakshamaam".' Passionate believer in inter-faith harmony as I am, I was surprised – and delighted – to see that she referred to Swami Chidananda as her 'Gurudev' – her highest Guru – and I wondered if perhaps Swami Chidananda was, like Swami Abshiktananda, a Christian. I was also puzzled by the meaning of 'Om Maria Rakshamaam' so I rang up my friend, the Sacred Heart Sister whom I've already mentioned, and asked her what it meant. To my surprise she told me that it meant God delivers (or protects) through Mary, so then I asked about Swami Chidananda. 'Was he a Hindu?' 'Of course,' was the some-what indignant reply. 'Who is he?' I asked. 'Who is he?' she replied, even more indignantly. 'The nearest thing to Jesus Christ on the face of the earth, that's who he is.' I was left full of gratitude and wonder that a former Parsi Sacred Heart religious should have as her great Guru a Hindu swami who taught her to say, 'God protects through Mary', a man who is himself a great saint.

At that moment, and ever since then, I felt that I was at one with the millions of souls throughout history, who have loved and honoured Our Lady – with saints like St Francis of Assisi, and St Bernard of Clairvaux, and yet also with Wordsworth and Byron, with Longfellow and Harriet Beecher Stowe, with Rumi and the Sufi mystics, and with the prophet Muhammad himself (in the Koran, Our Lady is held in the highest honour, and is frequently mentioned). Those words have now become an unchanging mantra for me.

These have been the two most significant experiences of my spiritual life, and I will be grateful for them to my dying day.

When I was a child a very dear and holy uncle of mine gave my brother and me an autograph book each. I remember him saying that in one he would write, 'God is Truth' and in the other, 'God is Love'. Before my brother could answer I said, 'Oh please, write, "God is Love" in mine.'

Today I would have to say, 'God is Love'; yes, indeed, but, like St Aelred of Rievaulx, I would also have to say, 'God is

Friendship', for amongst all the manifold blessings with which God has blessed me, though so unworthy, one of the greatest has been the gift of friendship. I am privileged to have an abundance of the most wonderful friends, and, like Marlowe, I too can say, 'These are my friends in whom I more rejoice, than does the King of Persia in this crown'.

So, as I look back over all the years that have gone, my heart is full of pride and gratitude for the whole procession of the noble company of my mentors and inspirers, who, in their several ways, taught and inspired me on my journey through life, and who now rest in the peace of God: my grandmother; Bishop Christopher and Lakdasa; Joost de Blank and memorably Edward Carpenter, worthy colleagues of each other at Westminster Abbey; Trevor Huddleston and Colin Winter, lovers of Africa and ardent fighters for its freedom; Father Wain and Donald Nicholl; and my beloved Mother Jane of Fairacres, my spiritual director until her death, someone whose presence I miss every day of my life.

I have always longed for the acknowledgment of our common humanity under God, and so I take great comfort from the words of Bishop Lakshman Wickremsinghe when he said in the second Lambeth Inter-Faith Lecture in 1978:

Now we see the goal of dialogue but darkly. In the realised realm of truth and righteousness, recorded in the last chapters of the Book of Revelation, we shall see face to face. The servants of God shall see him, who is Source, Guide and God of all that is, and adore. The riches of other streams of salvation will be drawn into that realm by the Divine Light that illumines and attracts. What is now hidden will be revealed. Until then we follow the path open to us in this era, and seek to have a foretaste of what mankind, in its fullness, can be. Then togetherness will enrich uniqueness, and uniqueness will illuminate togetherness. To that final dawn may the Father of all lead us.

And finally, as I move towards the close of my own journey in this wonderful and fascinating world of ours, I can only commend my soul to the mercy of God in the words of that prayer that over the centuries has been the final comfort for all sorts and conditions of men and women all over the world:

> Hail Mary, full of grace, the Lord is with thee.
> Blessed art thou among women
> and blessed is the fruit of thy womb, Jesus.
> Holy Mary, Mother of God,
> pray for us sinners, now and at the hour of our death.
> Amen.

Reflection 1

Bishop Christopher Robinson who was a member of the Delhi Brotherhood, which works with the poorest in Northern India, said, 'Remember . . . there is no such thing as a specifically Christian virtue, all the great virtues are universal; and *no* faith can claim a monopoly of them. There are Christ-like virtues, but those are usually to be found more often in non-Christians than in Christians.'

Discussion and Action

1. What do you learn of the Zoroastrian faith from Nadir?

2. What is the significance of the behaviour of Cyrus the King of Persia, who lived from approximately 590 to 529 BCE?

3. Meet someone from another faith, or visit the community centre of people of another faith. Listen, learn and also share.

Reflection 2

Archbishop Joost de Blank told Nadir to be a 'Voice of the Voiceless'.

STILLNESS AND STORM
IN SRI LANKA

Introduction

Sri Lanka today is a multi-religious, multi-racial and multi-lingual country. The Sinhala people are 74 per cent of the population, whilst Tamils are 18 per cent. There are also Moors, Malays and Burghers. The main religions are Buddhism, Hinduism, Christianity and Islam. Sixty-nine per cent of the people are Buddhist.

The tradition is that both the Sinhala and Tamil people went to Sri Lanka from India in about 500 BCE. The Sinhala people originated in north-eastern India, whilst the Tamil people orginated in south India. The Sinhala and Tamil people have shared the development of the country and have often worked together in the past. The Moors and Malays went to Sri Lanka later as traders. A second group of Tamils went to Sri Lanka in the nineteenth century, to work in the tea estates during the colonial era.

There were three main colonisations of Sri Lanka. The Portuguese were there from the early sixteenth century until the mid-seventeenth century. The Dutch followed the Portuguese and stayed until the eighteenth century. The British followed the Dutch, and they stayed until the country became independent in 1948. The main plantations established in the colonial era were tea, rubber and coconut. Much of the land was taken from the people and the country began to import some food. By the 1960s the prices of imports were rising whilst the prices of the exports were declining, and Sri Lanka began to borrow money and become a debtor nation.

The ethnic conflict, which developed after Sri Lanka became independent, was partly linked to the economic situation and partly to discrimination against the Tamil people after 1948. One example of this was the establishment of Sinhala as the official language in 1956. This was done perhaps to compensate for the advantages the British had given to the Tamil people. In 1976 the Tamils demanded a separate state, which was refused, and from that time the ethnic divisions and clashes have continued. The people of Sri Lanka continue to live in a violent situation, the economy has crumbled and development has gone into reverse. Sri Lanka is sadly but one example of a country living with an internal war in the twenty-first century. There are many more examples.

Reflection

Looking from this garden I see God
smiling in the golden fields
stooked harvest square.

But what of the harvest of hate
and anguished dread, the scarred and dead
whose lives and homes are burnt
as one burns spurned stubble;
in the field, the house, the street
where they have fallen on the ground
like seeds, what will be reaped?

O what a bitter wound within the nation,
what black hurricanes of desolation.
Why such awful vengeance?
When we cry out does God answer
only by his silence?
Or is his answer in the brave, just, kind,
who serve the plight of the fugitives,
not hiding from stark truth and grief
but seeking how to deal and bind
the sundered in one sheaf?

Olive Hitchock

There have been many responses to the ethnic divisions and violence which have afflicted Sri Lanka. I include only two examples. They represent many more.

Devasarana

In the early 1950s a young Anglican priest, previously with three village churches, moved to Devasarana north of Kurunegala, to begin an action-reflection movement in the context of Buddhist-Christian dialogue. Yohan Devananda took the title 'Sevaka' which put his leadership in the contemplative Christian ashram tradition, and a community grew with commitment to the lifestyle which rural people were practising. Thomas Merton visited Devasarana during his 'Asian Journey', and wrote, 'The buildings are all very simple; in fact they are nothing but the watchhouses, chicken runs, etc., that were there before. The chapel is in an open chicken house with a concrete floor. One sits on mats. The altar is a low table. The bronze lamps are Ceylonese. . . . The atmosphere of the place is quiet, open . . . it is certainly "poor" and "simple", a good example of what a monastic experiment in Asia should look like.'

The centre developed a collective farm as a starting point for entering the field of peasant organisation, and has joined in the development-justice-liberation movement. Later, in the face of ethnic conflicts and the civil war in the north, a thrust for peace grew quickly, and this led Yohan Devananda to be joint organising secretary of the World Solidarity Forum for Justice and Peace in Sri Lanka. The Forum's 1994 Memorandum on Peace-Making and Constitutional Reform is a contribution which has the backing of many leading clergy, both Buddhist and Christian, and interested politicians, including those in the UK.

Good Wishes House

Father Michael Rodrigo was someone who worked to bring the people of Sri Lanka together, through the example of his life and work in a village. He was felled by the bullet of a killer towards the end of the Mass he had just celebrated with his little community at Buttala. This murder while celebrating the Eucharist was to many of his friends reminiscent of the killing of Archbishop Oscar Romero of El Salvador.

Mike Rodrigo, born on 30 June 1927, was first a professor at the National Seminary of the Roman Catholic Church at Ampitiya from 1955 to 1971. He later served at the Centre for Society and Religion and in 1972 became the director of Sevaka Sevana in Bandarawela, which was the Badulla Diocesan Seminary set up by Bishop Leo Nanayakkara. Fr Mike was released by the same Bishop to live at Buttala in a community including himself, two sisters and a young Buddhist. 'Suba Seth Gedera', or Good Wishes House, was the name of the cottage in which Mike sought to commence a Buddhist-Christian dialogue and village awareness-raising in the area.

The choice of Buttala for this venture was significant. Buttala was in the area of Vellassa (meaning in Sinhala 'a hundred thousand rice fields'), which in the days of the Sinhala kings was the veritable rice bowl of the island. The people of Vellassa have had a tradition of rebellion and sturdy independence. The great rebellion of 1817 against the British, also based in the Vellassa region, was suppressed with annihilating thoroughness by the colonial government. Writing of these happenings, Fr Michael has remarked: 'There took place in the year 1818 unwonted reprisals against the peasantry – their tanks or reservoirs, their homes and all their possessions were destroyed. An imperialist power governing the island through a Christian governor brought to naught the work of generations of Buddhist peasants in one fell stroke. This event, seared into their memory and willy-nilly upheld in mind and imagination, even 165 years later produces in them a traumatic shock.'

Michael succeeded in establishing close rapport with the villagers and the youth in particular, and gave them a new understanding of what it meant to be a Christian and to be truly the Church in the village setting. He understood Buddhism and identified with village life, its culture and its poverty. He grasped the problems confronting the peasants. He intervened on behalf of the poor villagers and the workers of the multinational close by at Pelwatte. He was loved by the people.

Not unnaturally he was for that very reason seen as a threat to the vested interests of the area and to the *status quo*. Unfortunately, the absence of a movement to back him effectively in his witness, both at the local and national levels, made Michael vulnerable to the reactionary forces at work.

The quality of Mike's witness and its impact on the people he served cannot, however, be disputed. When the Buddhist villagers found his dead body lying on the ground, they reverently gathered up the pieces of his brain and the eyes which had fallen out and buried them in the garden, putting up two crosses to mark the spots. In doing so they said, 'These were the eyes which saw our condition and this is the brain that guided us. These were the most precious parts of the body and since we have them, Fr Michael still remains with us.'

Reflection

'Somehow I found Christ. I went to the village and was converted because he was present . . .' *Michael Rodrigo*

To Michael
For one brief moment, Michael,
in the Christian Church
of Lanka
rite and reality
became one.
When the gun roared,
ravaged your gentle face
and the deep dark engulfed you,
in that flash of light
the Temple veil was rent
and the Christ-event became clear
to the poor.

The Poor and Father Mike
His ambition
was not to be
a leader
of the poor.
No, he merely stood
beside them
till they discovered
their own potential.

He was not the voice
of the voiceless.
No, he merely stood
beside them
till they found
their own voice,
their own speech.
Basil Fernando

Discussion and Action

1. Discuss why Michael Rodrigo was accepted by the people of Buttala.

2. What do the lives of Yohan Devananda and Michael Rodrigo teach us about bringing people together and living in a multi-cultural and multi-faith society?

Prayer for Sri Lanka

Dear God,
   we pray for your loving presence
   in all the suffering situations of Sri Lanka.
We pray for the ordinary people
   who have lost their homes over more than twenty years.
We pray for those who have died,
   and especially for the children who have died.
We pray for the people of Jaffna
   who suffer isolation and deprivation.
We pray for members of the Government army
   and for members of the Tamil Tigers.
We pray for those who direct policy.
We give thanks for all those
   who are working for wisdom, understanding and peace.
Amen.

An Asian Way of
Celebrating Psalm 23

I met Harry Haas, a Dutch Roman Catholic priest, in the Woodlands community home in Bandarawela, 4,000 feet up in the hill country of Sri Lanka. The community house is painted brightly with flowers and there is a warm welcome and good locally grown food for visitors. Woodlands is the home of a network of groups all working on some aspect of the development of people side by side with the protection of the land. Organic farming is one important focus; another is the creative and fair development of the spice trade. The Uva spice factory is a colourful and odoriferous community centre run by local women who produce the many herbs and spices which are sold locally and all over the world. A nearby tea estate is encouraged at every level of its life, including the housing and working conditions of the workers and their children and the promotion and fair trading of the tea. There is a special focus on creative tourism, which encourages people to come to Sri Lanka for the benefit of the country and people, and not for their exploitation. The Link Language School is also part of the Woodlands Network. It is developing methods to build people's confidence in learning and using English. The growth and development of both individuals and communities is the aim of work in all areas of life in the Woodlands Network.

The Story of Eileen Candappa

Harry Haas

Eileen Candappa was born in 1923, into a Colombo Chitty family. The Chitties are neither Tamil nor Sinhalese. They also once came from India but they insist that they have deep roots in Sri Lanka. Today, they are a recognised ethnic minority which is mainly Christian and has English as the mother tongue. Their excellent cuisine is multi-cultural and they feel at ease in the East as well as the West.

Eileen migrated to the UK as a young adult – 'to see the world', as she liked to put it. Her excellent secretarial skills enabled her to find a job instantly. In London, she moved mainly with her multi-national extended family, and an inter-cultural community which included many English people. She wore a saree throughout her long life, improved her cooking ability, and kept English as her mother tongue.

From 1963 Eileen worked with me, first in Germany, where I was the Catholic national chaplain to international students. Her flat in Bonn was a rallying point for people from all over the world. Asian hospitality, Sri Lankan openness, listening and counselling were the trademarks of her 'wayside inn'.

Few European women, let alone Asian ones, were so involved with so many nationalities as Eileen Candappa. Soft-spoken but straightforward, Eileen made an impact wherever she went.

With me, she belonged to the team in charge of the 'Liturgical Night', a happy and captivating form of worship developed especially for the 'Evangelischer Kirchentag', a biennial national meeting of Lutherans in Germany. The Liturgical Night of 1973 in Dusseldorf was one of the elements which revived an almost defunct convention. Today, more than 100,000 participants make it difficult to find a suitable venue for the Kirchentag.

For a Kirchentag in Berlin, Eileen proposed her favourite Psalm 23, 'My shepherd is the Lord' as the theme. Her proposal was accepted without discussion. We decided to get together for a weekend and decide on the best way of acting the psalm out.

The easy acceptance of Eileen's proposal proved to be an excellent decision. Is there any psalm closer to the hearts of Christians of all churches and denominations than this one? However, at first, it was found to be culturally, and therefore spiritually, alien. The team members, Lutheran pastors and a few of their wives, were rather helpless when, in small groups, we were asked to take a sensitive approach to this classic of the psalms. Our sub-group grappled with 'You anoint my head with oil'. Easy to sing, but how to actually demonstrate its meaning was much harder. As a Catholic priest, I have been anointed and anointed others on many occasions, but never was my head anointed.

Eileen had a practical idea. She had Chinese Tiger Balm, which she had bought in Singapore and which she had in her bag. She was fond of this ointment as a medication. To put the Germans at their ease, I massaged their temples lightly with it. They all wanted to have that experience. Then we anointed each other's heads. Also, this anointing given and received was a revelation to me. I had associated ritual anointing more with spiritual power than with tenderness. Eileen shared her strength and tenderness with whomever she anointed better than any bishop or priest ever could.

When we presented our experience to the plenary session, all wanted to share it. Then it was decided to have the anointing as part of the Berlin Liturgical Night, when 8,000 people were expected to attend. Grass oil was chosen for the anointing in order to avoid anything with an overpowering perfume.

Eileen and I ruminated often about the way clumsiness and aloofness in that Berlin crowd gave way to tenderness and trust with the anointing.

However, that was not what made us see Psalm 23 from

an unexpected angle. It struck us that Jesus spoke so well of the good shepherd, unmistakably from intimate knowledge. But we know that he was a carpenter's son, probably himself trained in the trade. Did the shepherds who came for his birth disappear thereafter? Would they not have brought the child and his parents into safety, from oasis to oasis, from clan to clan? Did not Jesus' intimate knowledge of the shepherds' life stem from the family's time as refugees in the desert?

Once on this track, we came to the conclusion that those shepherds were not Jews or Arabs, but Bedouins. We understood the significance of this crossing of ethnic and cultural borders, as this was our profession. How can somebody who had seen the Light continue to contemplate his own dim lantern?

After Eileen had died in our house in Bandarawela, Sri Lanka, where we had stayed since 1983, I phoned the priest of the nearby Anglican Church of the Assumption. We had an Anglican service in the house. Hardly any Christians were present. Of course we sang Psalm 23, in English and Sinhala. I had asked the Anglican priest, a lively Sinhalese, to explain something about shepherds and sheep to the Buddhists present, in a country where sheep and shepherds are unknown. It was a tall order. He himself had apparently never given any thought to the matter. There are no water buffaloes, either, in Bandarawela, which is in the mountains, but everybody has seen them shepherded on the plains. And what about the mahout and his elephant?

So, with these illustrations and with God's help, the matter was resolved, as Eileen herself might have resolved it.

Reflection

The action of anointing was so much more powerful than the simple reading of the psalm, perhaps because it offered a

The Stilling of the Storm
Francis Hoyland

more vivid and dynamic experience of giving and being given, which brought people together in friendship and trust.

When Jesus was in a boat on the lake with his disciples in the storm, they were frightened but he, as on many other occasions in his ministry, was able to bring peace. The disciples panicked and allowed the storm to take control of them, whilst Jesus took control of the whole situation by extending his own inner peace to his surroundings.

'Jesus got into a boat, and his disciples went with him. Suddenly a fierce storm hit the lake and the boat was in danger of sinking. But Jesus was asleep. The disciples went to him and woke him up. "Save us, Lord," they said. "We are about to die!" "Why are you so frightened?" Jesus answered. "How little faith you have!" Then he got up and ordered the winds and the waves to stop, and there was great calm.' *Matthew 8:23-26*

Discussion and Action

1. Share experiences of meeting 'people of inner calm and peace' and of their influence on situations around them.

2. Share experiences of the crossing of ethnic and cultural borders which have led to the growth of trust and mutual service. Discuss why such experience may be powerful and enabling.

3. Identify an area in your community where there are borders to be crossed and new friends to be made, and make a commitment to do so.

LINKS OF DIFFERENCE
IN THE FAR EAST

Secrets and Shocks in Japan

Missionary activity was forbidden in Japan in the late sixteenth century and Christianity was forbidden altogether in 1637. When Japan became more open, and Christianity was allowed again, in the nineteenth century, it was discovered that Christians had kept their faith secretly through all the years of persecution. Crosses were hidden in mirrors and wooden carvings, including Buddhas. When I was invited to the museum where many of the carvings are now housed, at Oiso near Yokohama, we were also shown blocks of wood with relief carvings of Mary and Jesus. The reliefs were used for block printing so that suspected Christians could be asked to step on to the prints. They were killed if they refused. I was shown a wooden block with figures of a mother and child without faces. I was told that the Buddhist wood carvers had produced the blocks without faces to help the Christians in their time of trial, because they need not avoid treading on images without faces, and so could save their lives.

The Elizabeth Sanders home for children is next door to the museum at Oiso. The home was founded by a Japanese woman, Mikki Sawada, who became totally committed to its creation by accident. She was on a train journey when suddenly she was hit on the head by a parcel from the luggage rack. She opened the parcel to find that it contained the body of a baby. She alighted from the train a different woman. She found out more about the dead baby, and devoted her life to the foundation of a home for other abandoned children.

When America occupied Japan after the Pacific or Second World War, a number of illegitimate children were born to Japanese girls, fathered by GIs. The children were often abandoned, like the baby found in the parcel by Mikki Sawada. She responded to her 'shock' by working hard to raise money and land to found the home which was named after the English woman who gave some money for its development. I visited the home in the 1990s, many years after its foundation. It is a bright place, and still a home for children of all ages who have been deprived or left alone in life.

The people of the Kobe area faced shock followed by disaster when the earthquake struck early in 1995. I visited the Bishop of Kobe and his wife and realised that there was a heap of rubble where a building had once stood just across the footpath from their home. The bishop has written about what happened.

> The violent shaking was first vertical, followed by rapid horizontal movements. Shelves, cupboards and dressers fell over. I heard a loud noise and thought the building would collapse. . . . Finally the shaking stopped and we tried to find light in the darkness. My wife found a candle. We discovered that our daughter upstairs was all right. . . . The third floor of the building opposite our house was now at first-floor level and people were escaping out of the windows. Without metal saws or cutting torches the building could not be entered. Eventually we learnt that 18 had died. A two-storey building with tile roof, also nearby, collapsed. A woman was calling out for help. I broke a window and rescued her and brought her to our house. . . . Volunteers came from far and near with relief supplies. . . . Those who had not personally experienced the devastation of war, and had never been without water, light, heat, communication, food, clothing and shelter, felt deeply the impact of the disaster . . .

Some people had been made homeless for the second time by the earthquake, the first time being when the atomic bomb was dropped on Hiroshima during the Pacific or Second World War.

I spent some time in Hiroshima, a huge and modern city with wide streets and shopping precincts. It is the home of Mazda cars, and also of the memorial park to those who died in the bombing. It is a memorial for the many people who were swallowed up in a red hot cage, sacrificed by all sides. I read the story of the bombing and of the campaign for world peace. I saw the everyday things, the pots and pans, the clothes and school bags and books.

The memorial to the children who died includes a girl with a crane, a symbol of hope for the future. It is based on the story of a real girl, who survived the bomb but died later, of leukaemia. As she lay in hospital she made hundreds of paper cranes, never giving up hope for the future.

Reflection 1

'Lord, make us vessels of your peace.'

This was the prayer adopted by the Nippon Seikokai, the 'Holy Catholic Church of Japan' (Anglican Church), for its centenary celebrations in 1987. The Church, by acknowledging its share in the history of Japan, has found itself strengthened as a witness of reconciliation. The treasure of God is carried in vessels of clay.

Discussion and Action

1. The story of the Buddhist help to the Japanese Christians is a challenge to those who live in inter-faith Britain, where Christianity is the majority and established religion and where people of other faiths may face problems, especially of being accepted. Find out more and develop friendship.

2. Find out where people of faith are suffering because of their faith in the world today. Pray and where possible do something to help.

The Ten Lepers
Francis Hoyland

Reflection 2

'As Jesus made his way to Jerusalem, he went along the border between Samaria and Galilee. He was going into a village when he was met by ten men suffering from a dreaded skin disease. They stood at a distance and shouted, "Jesus, Master! Take pity on us." Jesus saw them and said to them, "Go and let the priests examine you." On the way they were made clean. When one of them saw that he was healed, he came back, praising God in a loud voice. He threw himself to the ground at Jesus' feet and thanked him. The man was a Samaritan.

'Jesus said, "There were ten men who were healed; where are the other nine?"' *Luke 17:11-17*

Discussion

Remember what happened to Mikki Sawada and share personal experiences of shock leading to new life.

Links of Difference:
Japan and Papua New Guinea

When I was invited to the home of the retired Anglican Archbishop of Japan, Christopher Kikawada, I noticed a wall-hanging made of beads in the sitting room. It was a gift from Papua New Guinea, given during a visit of reconciliation made by the archbishop on the fiftieth anniversary of the execution by Japanese soldiers of England's Vivian Redlitch and other missionaries during the Pacific War.

The Nippon Seikokai has worked very hard for reconciliation following the atrocities committed during the war. Bishop Raphael Kajiwara wrote, 'I would like to express our regretful sorrow for past history of fifty years ago in Papua New Guinea and other Southern Pacific areas . . . where people were killed by the violence of the Japanese soldiers . . . As a Japanese, I confess our deep sorrow . . . and I am asking for your friendly benevolence to forgive our past . . . hoping to deepen our future mutual understanding and friendship . . .'

Lucian Tapiedi was a Papua New Guinean who died for his faith during the Pacific War. He is one of ten twentieth-century martyrs whose statues have been placed above the west front of Westminster Abbey.

The Australians who were in Papua New Guinea during the war named their PNG colleagues 'the fuzzy-wuzzy angels' because of their bravery, especially as stretcher-bearers. Today a first aid post at Kebara stands near to the scene of some of the bitterest jungle fighting.

In 1997 there was another threat, in the form of a cyclone, when everyone had to flee. The cyclone was followed by an eight-month drought and bush fires. Yet, as soon as the rain began to fall, people were out planting and building. The building included the new church, for the earlier one had been destroyed in the cyclone. The people did the fundraising, logging and preparing of the timber for the church.

Over 80 per cent of the people in Papua New Guinea live in villages and live by subsistence farming. Most of the people have quickly decaying housing, poor transport, difficult access to education and healthcare. Two hundred and thirty children die each week from preventable illnesses. No wonder the people are tempted to sell the trees and the minerals. Logging and mining companies are keen to pay what seems to them a large amount but is in fact only a fraction of either the profit to the company or the cost to the people. When the companies pull out, they leave desolation.

Reflection

Bishop Tevita Talanoa is now the bishop of Dogura. He walks everywhere, sometimes for two days or more and sometimes starting out at 4 am. He was born in Tonga and educated in Fiji. One of his brothers was a pearl diver.

He faced a time of crisis in 1989 when he was a priest on Bourgainville Island. The Bourgainville army tried to secede from Papua New Guinea and also to gain compensation for the use of their land. They also closed the giant copper mine. A guerrilla war followed and in 1990 the government forces left the island and many other people also left, until the Honiara Peace Declaration was signed in 1991. A peace deal was signed in 1998. Over the period of war about 10,000 lives were lost. Bishop Tevitha stayed on the island throughout the war with his wife Winifred and his family. Finally he had a congregation of six people, the soldiers were coming and his bishop asked him to leave. He will always remember the night he and his sons burnt the church altar and furnishings, before leaving.

The situation for the indigenous Indians of South America is, like that of the people of Papua New Guinea, very serious. Communities such as the Yanomani, Kaiowa and Makuxi in Brazil are suffering at the hands of miners, loggers and farmers.

Some of the activities of the miners, loggers and farmers are depriving the Indian people of their traditional livelihoods and also damaging the land.

The Indian people are deeply involved with the land in the spiritual sense; they have tended it for thousands of years and are destroyed when they see it torn up. They see themselves as the trustees of the land, which they believe cannot be bought or sold.

Discussion and Action

1. Discuss possibilities for sustainable methods for the use of land and resources in Papua New Guinea, Brazil and other similar places around the world. Consider the possibility of the local people processing their own natural resources.

2. Go to see the statues of the martyrs on the west front of Westminster Abbey. Find out more about each one.

3. Consider the time of crisis Bishop Tevitha faced. Is it ever possible to prepare for such times?

4. Take inspiration from the Japanese Christian example. Where is reconciliation work most needed in our world today? How might we help?

Letters from Vietnam

William Allen was a teacher of English in a polytechnic centre in HA Long, in Vietnam, for most of the 1990s. The demand for people to speak English, the worldwide language of business, is growing daily, and very soon it will be taught in every school. William lived in three rooms in the single-storey college. His flat was cool, tiled, clean and well furnished. He had a view of the bay, which little by little diminished as it was dug up to provide materials for all the new buildings. He cycled the five kilometres to his classes of teachers and school-leavers. He also taught in a school for gifted children, and spent his Sunday afternoons working on pronunciation and communication skills with a class of four, including the vice-chair of the provincial people's committee, Mrs Hong Khuong. Mrs Hong Khuong holds a very important post and sits side by side with a nightwatchman. Their relationship is one of equals. After three years William moved to teach English to professional people, including engineers, vets, agriculturalists and bureaucrats. They all needed English for their work.

William committed himself to Vietnam and the people. He learnt the language, made friends and stayed in families. He wrote regular letters from Vietnam to his family and friends from which a vivid picture of the country and people emerges.

Life is much slower in Vietnam than in the West. The number of cars is growing – the ex-army jeeps are being replaced by Toyotas and Nissans – but most people have bicycles, even in the cities. Bells, horns and hooters are not an expression of annoyance but simply add to the atmosphere. Saigon is rather characterless and very modern whilst Hannoi is a beautiful city of lakes and pagodas, parks and pavement cafés. There is great commercial activity and at times it seems that everyone is out on the streets selling something. Old men sit at street corners with a few homemade tools and a couple of decanters of butane, trying to make a living from refilling lighters. Many people have opened their homes as shops. They have doors which fold back to reveal the entire room, which includes cabinets full of biscuits and bottles of fizzy drink. The room also includes the TV, the bed and the family shrine. The washing of hair and of pots and pans normally takes place on the street. Hanoi has a street for everything, including silk street, stationery street, film processing street, electronics street and army surplus street. Every night the streets are swept clean. The drab concrete is mostly covered by bright advertisements and new buildings are going up everywhere.

Construction work is going on in all corners of the country, in the villages as well as in the towns. There are piles of sand in almost every place, and little shacks stand dwarfed by new multi-storey brick houses. There is 'ceaseless and rapid change amidst the permanent beauty of the land and the tranquillity of the people'. There are many hotel schemes around the coastline and in the cities. The roads are full of lorries carrying building materials. Trees are being cut down to build houses and also to make furniture. There is recent awareness of the danger to the country of the loss of the forests. A Thai businessman was forced by the government to plant a forest the same size as the golf course he built outside Ho Chi Minh.

The Vietnamese countryside is prospering now. The 1988 land reforms transferred land-tenure, though not ownership, from the collectives to families. Since then rice production has doubled and Vietnam is the world's third largest exporter. The country people in both the North and the South are very friendly and welcome visitors into their homes where there is a relaxed atmosphere, usually with children scampering around.

There is a great awareness of the war, especially in the South where the Museum of War is a very chilling place with its photographs of atrocities and even jars containing Agent Orange deformed foetuses. Forty kilometres from Saigon is the maze of tunnels, sometimes three storeys deep, and including living, medical and command rooms and even arsenals, which gave the Vietnamese guerrilla army access to Saigon, the US bases and every village over an enormous area. Parts of the tunnels are now a museum.

Some of those who left Vietnam during and after the war are now returning, especially as there are no longer the Hong Kong camps, where many people spent several years whilst waiting for the opportunity to go to other countries. The European Community provides help for people when they return to Vietnam, including education, but it is not easy for them to settle and to be accepted. Many of the former 'boat people' have settled and made new lives all over the world, including the UK.

Reflection

'I left Vietnam when I was 14, in 1978. I escaped with six younger brothers and sisters. . . . While it was still dark one early morning we started to walk out towards the sea. . . . There was a little boat that would take us to a big boat. . . . As we got on to the big boat there was much shouting and screaming, looking for relatives and friends. I couldn't see my parents or elder sister . . . we were all sent down to the cabin. We didn't have a thing with us, except for a bag of shoes. My mother had all the clothes and the money. . . . Our destination was Malaysia, and then England decided to accept us. When we arrived in England it was very cold and we lived in the middle of the countryside. . . . I eventually went to college to take O-levels. The others went to school. . . . My parents arrived in England in 1981. Now I am a nursery nurse and have a mortgage on my house. Life is coming good, but my experiences will never leave me.' *Lan Nguyen*

Discussion and Action

1. What do you find worrying and what do you find hopeful about developments in Vietnam today?

2. Have you met any of the Vietnamese people who came to settle, perhaps in South London or in your home area? Make an effort to meet people and to learn about their lives and work.

LISTEN TO AFRICA

Zambia and AIDS

Most people in Zambia, like most people in many countries of Africa at the beginning of the twenty-first century, have been touched personally by AIDS. AIDS is rampant in every sector of society. It is especially bad on the Zambian Copperbelt, perhaps because there are so many young people living in crowded and poor conditions.

Poor conditions favour the spread of AIDS, including the poor medical services, lack of education, the desperation that leads to prostitution and the despair that leads to drug abuse.

Men are much more likely to spread AIDS, but young women, aged 15 to 25 years, are most likely to contract it.

A Zambian child of 15 years has a 60 per cent likelihood of dying of AIDS-related illness.

One woman in Lusaka told of how her daughter had married a man who, unknown to her, was HIV positive. They had a child, but within a few years the whole family, having developed AIDS, was dead. This woman's family was not unusual.

There is a rapid and very worrying growth in the number of orphans in Zambia. The elderly are looking after young children, and sometimes the children are 'looking after' themselves. Many young children are now living on the streets, joining the huge band of street children in the big cities of the developing world. In Zambia's cities the children are more fortunate than some, because often they do have somewhere to sleep at night. They sometimes sell things or they beg. Most of them cannot think of going to school, because they would have to buy books and uniforms, and to pay fees.

When children do go to primary school the conditions in most areas are now far from reasonable. One primary school, in Fiwila, which is out in the bush in Central Zambia, was started in the 1920s. The children make long journeys to the school, and stay in dormitories with their own sleeping mats

217

and a meagre supply of food. The conditions are appalling, with very few pit latrines and extremely basic cooking and supervision. The local health centre is ill-equipped and staffed, with only a medical orderly, two nurse midwives and an enrolled nurse for a huge area. The local people are now making efforts to grow some traditional food crops, including maize, millet, pumpkins and beans. A shop has also been opened.

Father Samuel Sipeko has kept a diary during his ministry in Fiwila.

> I passed through the school grounds. I saw two children, one a walking matchstick, almost nothing between bones and skin; the other losing weight, also weak, returning home after school, hungry. . . . Then, near the garage I saw a girl, probably nine or ten, drinking water from the tap there. I looked at her, she was weak, hungry, had sleepy aimless eyes.

Zambia is facing the reality of AIDS, as are many African countries now.

Uganda has led the way in this. It was the first country to tackle AIDS openly with the result that HIV prevalence and sexually transmitted diseases have dropped. Tanzania is now giving out very detailed advice to help people. The development of good materials for education is encouraged, especially from youth to youth.

The newspapers in Zambia are bringing attention to the problems and there is publicity for organisations offering sex education. One way of reaching those who can't read or write is through drama.

The Church in Africa is playing its part in combating AIDS. It was widely noticed when the Roman Catholic Archbishop of Namibia said on television, 'AIDS is not a sin.'

In Zambia the churches are directly involved every time someone dies. The collection at the funeral service normally goes to the bereaved family and the church may provide a coffin and transport. Churches are helping orphans in many ways, including the giving of food and clothing, education and even a badly needed place to play.

The Western World may help by tackling the poverty of Zambia and of other poor countries, which is becoming more terrible every day. There are now more than a billion people in the world living in absolute poverty, which means that they have less than 65 pence per day. Thirty-five thousand children die every day because they are poor.

Reflection

How is the victory over poverty to be won?
How is the gap between the rich
and the poor nations of the world to be closed?
How can the nations of Africa
begin to trade in manufactured goods
as well as agricultural produce?
Christians must come to grips
with this complex subject of international economics.
Sympathy is not enough,
for in this area of life,
love without justice is an impossibility.
Written in 1971 by Jonathon Chileshe

Discussion and Action

1. Discuss the situation of the rapidly increasing band of AIDS orphans in Zambia. Make a list of the signs of hope for an improvement in the situation. Suggest ways of linking in with the signs of hope for a future for the orphans.

2. Find out about Target 2015, to halve world poverty by 2015. This is the goal of the world's governments.

3. Read the annual 'State of the World's Children' report which is published by UNICEF and which makes it clear that the poverty of children is increasing daily. Added to the normal diseases and health hazards children face are war and the HIV virus which affects five young people every minute.

The Act of Giving Is Greater than the Gift

Ailsa Moore

In 1966 I was living and teaching in Nigeria, in a boarding school situated in a small village some 50 miles from Lagos. At the time, I was running the Student Christian Movement in the school and usually about 40 or so students took part on a Sunday.

For a change, and as an educational visit, I decided to take the group to see a small Cheshire Home near to Lagos. This home was run by a remarkable Nigerian woman. She looked after twelve young people who were affected by various mental or physical problems. In Nigeria, it was unusual in those days to find a place like this one. Many of the disadvantaged would be found on the streets. I felt that seeing this rather wonderful place would be an uplifting experience for the students at my school.

Before we left for the visit, I suggested that everyone who was able to could take some small gift – a few sweets or biscuits. The students had little of their own, so making a small sacrifice for others worse off than themselves would be a worthwhile experience.

We boarded the wagon and set off. The visit was obviously successful. The students were unusually subdued as we were about to leave. I suggested that we put our small gifts on the table. We did this and the eyes of the residents lit up. As we were walking out of the door, one of my youngest pupils came to me with tears in his eyes, saying that he had brought nothing to give. I told him not to worry; that the people there would be happy with what we had brought.

But the boy was not satisfied. He hesitated, then took off his beautiful new sandals and placed them on the table. What

The Feeding of the Five Thousand
Francis Hoyland

a gift! For the rest of the term he would be without shoes. I walked out of the home in my shoes, with my arm round the shoulders of my barefoot 'teacher'.

Reflection

The boy stood at the crossroads of uncertainty and in making his choice he entered the path of generosity and love.

'Jesus went up a hill and sat down with his disciples. . . . Jesus looked round and saw that a large crowd was coming to him, so he asked Philip, "Where can we buy enough food to feed all these people?" Another of his disciples, Andrew, said, "There is a boy here who has five loaves of barley bread and two fish. But they will certainly not be enough for all these people." . . . Jesus took the bread, gave thanks to God, and distributed it to the people who were sitting there. He did the same with the fish and they all had as much as they wanted . . . they filled twelve baskets with the pieces left over . . .' *John 6:3-13*

Discussion and Action

When have we struggled with a choice of whether to be generous or not? What influenced our decision?

Make a new decision to be brave and generous in some area of your life.

A Glimpse of Family Life
in a South African Township

In 1997 Rachel stayed with her sister Eleanor in a family
home in a township near to Johannesburg.

The first thing I noticed when we arrived there was that
people spent more money on their fences than on their
houses. However, once behind the fences the people were
very friendly. It was strange being the only white people
there, but we soon got used to it. We were amazed by
how forgiving everyone was; as white people we could
have symbolised repression. One funny thing was that in
the church the younger children were staring at us in
amazement, and coming up to us to stroke our funny
coloured skin and hair! Soon we were taught a few words
in Xhosa, Zulu and Southern Sotho, which created much
amusement.

Much of our time at home was spent watching the
television. We became addicts of *Jam Alley*, a programme
about pop music, and of the various American soaps.
There is still a lot of television which is blatantly sexist
and racist, like the cartoons in Afrikaans which, without
fail, portray the black people as bad guys. Another activity
which took up quite a lot of time at home was preparing
and eating food. We all shared the work, under the supervision of Beauty, the mother of the family. We made vast
quantities of food for the two main meals of the day. The
breakfasty meal had lots of different kinds of meat, rice,
eggs and bread, all washed down with South African tea
and fizzy drinks. Everywhere we went people would get
out the bottles of fizzy drinks, collected from a small shop
behind the bars a few streets away. An old blind woman
living in a house made out of cardboard and corrugated

iron gave us drinks although she was terribly poor. Another meal was at the house of a church member in a leafy suburb, in a huge house with a swimming pool.

We were not allowed to go outside the main gates alone. Next to the house was a field with cows in it. Running through the field was a stream where people used to get water, which was filled with naked small boys jumping and splashing. Up the road there was a shop and a hairdresser. Both of these were part of people's houses. The hairdresser wanted to cut our hair, so he could get experience of non-Afro hair. We were driven to the post office, which was a very bare building with a counter. To do the main shopping we had to drive out of the township to Springs, where everything seemed very cheap to us but, for the local people, everything was harder and harder to afford.

People were happy to share with us, to make us feel at home and to tell stories of their past. Things had been tough and in many ways still are, but they live with great optimism for a better future, whilst retaining a realistic view. I noticed that those with a better standard of living were more dissatisfied with it than those who had nothing.

Reflection 1

Rachel wrote, 'I noticed that those with a better standard of living were more dissatisfied with it than those who had nothing.'

Discussion and Action

Identify some of the ingredients of the happy family life Rachel and Eleanor shared with Beauty and her family in the township.

Discuss some of the lessons for interracial harmony which others may learn from the black people of South Africa.

Make a plan to put the new insights into practice.

Reflection 2

People will build houses and live in them themselves;
they will not be used by someone else;
they will plant vineyards and enjoy the wine;
it will not be drunk by others.
Like trees, my people will live long lives.
They will fully enjoy the things that they have worked for.
Isaiah 65

Their Lives Go On

The life of Biko and those like him,
lost in the struggle for dignity,
the lives of the slaves thrown to the sharks
or of those whipped and worked to the ground.

The lives of those brutally cut short
by greedy Man in his quest for wealth,
in confrontations where poor helpless souls
were only viewed as stepping stones or obstacles
to be used or disposed of at will.

Their lives go on,
their blood speaks loud and clear
to give hope to millions,
for God will avenge their blood.

The lives go on,
of those whose only crime
was to raise a voice of conscience
for sharing what they believed in their hearts as truth.

The lives go on of those whose only
concern was for Humanity,
the right of every man to his dignity,
the right to be what God made him to be.
Victoria Amediku

Tantyi and Town (Distant View)

A racked house
faces me boldly.
Ponds of water here and there
make one screw one's nose.

Brown, rusty – most houses;
paint here and there.
White smoke tries unsuccessfully
to conceal the houses from heaven.
Dark, heavy clouds hover above Tantyi.

Foamy white clouds dance about town;
all the houses are white.
Did it snow over there?
I wish it would snow here too!
Lungile Lose (High school student)

Photo: Simon Curl

Art Student in a South African Shanty Town

Reflection

Many people do not have a deep-rooted home. Even those who have to be away from home, for work or other reasons, are lonely and would welcome friendship. 'At Christmas' was written in London by Janan Saab from Lebanon.

At Christmas

I miss my children,
my home, my country,
I miss the sea
with its waves,
I miss the sunshine
with its shining rays
glittering
on the whitely dressed
mountain landscapes.

I miss my friends,
my relatives,
myself
when I was living among my folks
and felt right.
I miss what was
Christmas for me.
It doesn't seem right
with no family
nearby.

Learning and Doing in Tanzania

Monica Mlemeta is a secretary in the Diocese of Mount Kilimanjaro. She has a son, Shadrak, and is married to Kedmon, an Anglican priest in charge of the cathedral in Arusha.

The Diocese of Mount Kilimanjaro, where Monica and Kedmon work, focuses on work with young people. It runs schools at every level, and also Sunday schools and youth clubs where the drama and singing are famous throughout East Africa.

Julius Nyerere was the first President of Tanzania. His vision in the Arusha Declaration of 1967 was of a future of freedom, equality and dignity for all the people of Tanzania. In the main entrance to the Arusha School there is a statement by Nyerere addressed to all those who will receive education in Tanzania, comparing them to 'the man who has been given all the food in a starving village in order that he might have the strength to bring supplies back from a distant place. If he takes this food and does not bring help to his brothers and sisters he is a traitor.' The statement goes on to directly challenge those who will be educated: 'Similarly, if any of the young men and women who are given an education by the people of this republic adopt attitudes of superiority, or fail to use their knowledge to help the development of this country then they are betraying our union . . .'*

The Anglican secondary school in Magila is in the Diocese of Zanzibar and Tanga. It has grown up as a place of respect for pupils of all faith traditions as well as for all the Christian denominations. The main groups, apart from the Anglicans, are Roman Catholics, Pentecostalists and Muslims. All the groups have their own meetings and worship. The pupils lead

* See also *Ujamaa: Essays on Socialism*, Julius Nyerere (OUP, 1974)

worship and regular discussion groups on issues facing the country and people.

The school is at 'the place of the cross' because the early missionary, Dr Krapf, who later went to Mombasa and began the Christian mission to Kenya, carved a cross on a tree here. The piece of the tree is now part of a cross at the entrance to the school. Magila was the first permanent nineteenth-century Anglican mission station.

The Story of Giver and Faith

Monica Mlemeta

Twenty-nine years ago, at the little village where I was born, and where I lived for twenty-two years, I was a pupil at a primary school. At this school there were two important men named Mr Giver and Mr Faith. The school was very poor. Most of the people in the village did not know the importance of education, particularly Mr Faith. It was Mr Giver who was the leader in the village.

At school, we used to sit on stones because there were no chairs and desks. Our school uniforms were soon torn because of sitting on the stones from eight o'clock in the morning until four o'clock in the afternoon when we left the school.

One day, Mr Faith came to the school. He did not care about the bad situation of pupils writing on the ground, seated on stones, and teachers sitting on boxes. He was quite rich compared to others in the village. He went away to continue praying and blaming problems on rich people.

After a week, Mr Giver visited the school. The teachers told him that Mr Faith had visited the week before. Mr Giver asked if Mr Faith had seen the situation of the school, and, if so, what comments and contributions he had made. Teachers told him that he was very pleased with the school and had promised to pray that God would do something for its problems. Now, Mr Giver was not rich as Mr Faith was, but Mr Giver was hardworking and honest.

Seeing the situation, he gave the teachers his ideas on how they might improve the situation. Accordingly they decided to call a meeting of parents and friends to have a fundraising project. That was the first meeting in that village and school since the school had started twenty years earlier.

Parents and others were excited to be invited to come, and everybody looked forward to seeing what would happen. Mr Faith came, but because the meeting aimed at encouraging contributions for the school, he was not happy at all. During the fundraising talk, Mr Giver promised that he would provide facilities for the teachers' office and also chairs for the pupils. After hearing about the contributions of Mr Giver, there was quiet as everybody waited to hear what the richest man in the village, Mr Faith, would contribute. After a long silence, Mr Faith at last spoke. He promised that he would offer his prayers to add to all their good ideas and their offers of money and facilities for the school.

Soon, the school had new desks, chairs, a blackboard and other facilities. At that time, I was in class four. I have said that Mr Faith was a rich man in the village. Beside that, he had a big family and sixteen children. Because he was not ready to contribute money to the school funds he did not send any of his children to school.

Fifteen years later, the school was thriving and in very good condition. Mr Faith was jealous of the development of the school without his help and he was always challenging Mr Giver about what was being done. He spent so much time doing this that he forgot to pray any more. In time he became a poor man, eaten up by jealousy and envy. Mr Giver continued to be a hard worker, helping the school and the poor people in the village. He became a faithful and respected man.

When I left my little village, Mr Faith had grown poor and Mr Giver had grown rich in the love of the people. I remembered the scriptures which said, 'Faith without works is dead', and, 'By their deeds ye shall know them'.

Reflection

How alien it is to people in the Western World to think of children sitting on stones at school as Monica Mlemeta did. What a remarkable achievement the people made to build Monica's school up from almost nothing. What an open and generous man Mr Giver was.

Julius Nyerere was a distinguished pioneer of education for all his people, an inspiration for the whole world.

Discussion and Action

1. Does education contribute towards unity and working together in our societies, or does it lead to differences and divisions?

2. Is it possible for the vision of Nyerere, that education should be for service and not for self-development and gain, to be the inspiration and expectation of our pupils and students in the West? Is this desirable, and, if so, how would you work towards it, in your own life and for others?

3. Is the Magila School, where all faiths and traditions are respected and given space, a good model for other schools in other countries?

The Story of an Old Man, John Lewis Mlanga

Told by his son Columbus

My father was born in 1908 in Handeni, in a village called Kwanjuno. This village is a few miles away from Handeni District Office.

He was born into a big family of ten children. He was the only one who was educated, and then he had to support the children of his sisters and brothers. When we children were growing up, we lived together with our cousins. There were about twenty children in our home, for whom my father was responsible, when I was growing up.

After my father had married my mother, they stayed in various places. Because my father was a teacher he was often transferred to different places and that is why they kept moving. At last, in 1956, my father decided to settle in Kideleko in the Tanga region, because he was doing a lot of building work in that area. As time went on, he was happy to see all the schools, hospital and churches which he had played a big part in building.

After he finished school, my father learnt many skills; among them, carpentry, building and masonry. He learnt something of veterinary medicine as well, and when he left school, he became a teacher and taught carpentry, building and the care of animals. During his working life, he did many things. He built a mission secondary school at Kideleko in Tanga region in Handeni district. The mission centre was called UMCA (Universities Mission to Central Africa) Kideleko. He also built another school, St Paul's Secondary School.

When he had been working for a long time, gaining experience, and being obedient to his superior, he was chosen to go to Kilimanjaro region where there was a school teaching the making of roof tiles. My father went there and learnt to make tiles for roofing houses. He became the first man in Tanga to master this skill. When he was building secondary schools at Kideleko, he was able to build from the foundations to the roof. He supervised brick-making, built the walls, put in the window and door-frames and the roof till the whole building was completed.

Together with others, my father built the first missionary church in Handeni, UMCA Kideleko Church. This church was a big one and very long. It was roofed with grass. I remember this church very well because I was baptised in it and it remained there while I was growing up. However, time went on and in the early 1960s this church was pulled down and my father, and others, built a model church in 1965, similar to others, roofed with timber and iron sheets. It was a very beautiful church.

So my father built churches as well as schools. Among the ten schools that he built were Kwekibo primary in 1958, Kimbe primary in 1959 and after this a bigger primary school at Kwakonje. This particular school was made with burnt bricks; the others with cement bricks.

The brick-built school looked beautiful. They did not plaster, so you can see all the bricks. It looked as smart as any other brick building. After that, he went to Manga and built another school. Later, in the 1960s, he built a mission dispensary in Kwachage district. I remember this well because I helped my father as a labourer.

By this time I was growing and I wanted to know what my father was doing. This is why he took me with him and allowed me to help him. I really enjoyed all this and I could see that the work was hard and sometimes dangerous. I really admired my father for the work he did.

In the Kideleko area, together with others, he built a big hospital which had fifty buildings, all roofed with iron sheets. Some of the buildings were made with burnt bricks, some with stones and cement. These building are still there and I think they will remain for a hundred years to come.

Throughout their lives, my father and mother were farming in addition to my father's teaching and building work. Also, another project which my father started while he was teaching at St Paul's, Kideleko, was a bakery. He sold bread in the village, and to the secondary school. He had many customers.

My father retired in 1975 and he died in 1993 when he was 85 years old. My mother died in 1989 when she was 63.

Bishop Edward Steere, who is buried in Zanzibar Cathedral, was a predecessor of Columbus's father, and rather like him. He set up a printing press and translated the New Testament and the Prayer Book into Swahili. He also built churches and schools, he learnt the art of brick-making himself and joined in the work whenever possible. He also learnt wheel-making, worked at the improvement of farming and developed a laundry in Zanzibar. Most famously, he directed the building of Zanzibar Cathedral, and celebrated the first Eucharist there on Christmas Day 1880. He was a pioneer in the development of appropriate technology, one example being his design of the vault of the cathedral of pounded coral and Portland cement.

The Zanzibar Cathedral of Christ the King was built on the site of the former slave market and the high altar stands where the auctions of the slaves took place. The font stands over the tunnel where the blood of the children who were killed because they were too weak to work drained away to the sea.

Reflection

Columbus's father had a lot in common with Edward Steere, though he was unknown and Bishop Steere was well known. Both men did such a lot in their lives, working for the benefit of others, offering examples of what was possible and providing symbols for the future of the people.

Discussion and Action

1. The Cathedral of Christ the King in Zanzibar is still a powerful symbol of the hope of freedom and fulfilment for the people. Make a list of other symbols, in other countries, which have the capacity to raise people's hopes and to give them courage to pray and to work for each other and for the wider world. Where are new symbols needed?

2. What would you work ceaselessly for in and with your community?

One small example of a community project was the building of a fishpond for the village of Lewa in the Usambara Mountains near to Korogwe. The fishpond had been planned a year before it was built, but a member of the community had been killed in a road accident and the work had been stopped. A visiting group from the UK gave the people the energy to return to their vision, and to dig out the hole, in the centre of the village, where the fishpond would be. It was a very long way from the mountainside to the pond. The channel had to be dug down the mountainside, through the bush and under a road before entering the village. When the digging began, the people came, and joined in, until soon the whole village was at work. Some of the women joined the digging whilst others prepared delicious meals for everyone, singing and sharing stories as they worked. Spirits rose and the channel was dug quickly, including the very complicated crossing of the road which was tackled successfully. Some of the workers even climbed the mountain behind the camp when the work was complete. The village bell rang and the way was cut for the water to enter the pond, symbolic of the success of the community efforts and of the hope for the future, of a pond full of fish and of a community which would share its vision with other communities.

The Story of Livingstone Mpalanyi Nkoyoyo

The story of Livingstone Mpalanyi Nkoyoyo has been written by Dunstan Bukenya and James Kaye.

I have known Dunstan and his wife Phebe for many years. Phebe is a nurse and leader of the movement for family life and loyalty in Uganda. Her work is vital for the future of the country, because family life, so central to African society, is under threat, especially since the AIDS epidemic has resulted in the deaths of many from the middle age groups, leaving thousands of orphans. Grandparents may currently find themselves responsible for huge numbers of grandchildren. Phebe is working so that good family life, with love and care for children, may be encouraged and also, in many cases now, recreated.

Dunstan is an Anglican priest and a lecturer at the Christian university in Makono. Dunstan and Phebe have often given generous hospitality and an introduction to their country to groups from Christians Aware who have gone out to visit and work in Uganda. They are usually the first people the visitors see when they emerge from the airport at Entebbe and the last people they see before they return home.

Ann Foat joined one group in the mid-1990s, a decade after President Museveni came to power and gave Uganda the peace and hope it had not known for more than two decades. Ann wrote of her time in a family home in Kampala:

> Breakfast was a generous meal of tropical fruit, toast and eggs. We discussed women's education, the problems of bringing up children and marriage and family life in a tribal and also multi-faith society. . . . Before lunch I washed some clothing out in the backyard . . . then we walked around the neighbourhood in a fast-growing part

of Kampala, situated on a hill slope amid the large and beautiful flowering trees. Brick-built houses are now springing up . . . most gardens boasted their banana patch, which every woman should have. We turned down the potholed and very dusty main road to the market area, full of shacks and stalls trading household essentials: matoke, bananas, pineapples, eggs, meat, bars of soap, jerry cans to carry water. . . . On the way home there was the daily power cut – electrical supplies are erratic. . . . The usual chaotic traffic jams were made worse by a cloud-burst, and torrential rain made the driving hazardous. . . . When we arrived home we enjoyed supper of meat stew, groundnut sauce, yams served with the staple food of steamed matoke or plantain, followed by tropical fruit. The day closed with family prayers.

I first met Dunstan when he was invited to England for the Dunstan Millennium in 1988* and joined a pilgrimage I helped to organise. We walked from Glastonbury to Canterbury, along the Pilgrim's Way. The ten days or so were an enjoyable holiday for most of us from the UK and USA, many from churches dedicated to Dunstan. Dunstan himself found the whole enterprise strange and very difficult. He came from a continent where people do not walk for pleasure, but to stay alive, to collect food and water, to go to school and to work. He had to borrow the walking boots he wore, which were far from comfortable; and also the sleeping bag which was not big enough for such a tall man. He remained cheerful throughout his experiences, ever ready to learn new, and to him rather odd, ways, always at the centre of energetic discussions, always present for times of prayer and meditation.

* The Dunstan Millennium was the 1988 celebration of 1,000 years since the death of Dunstan.

The Bishop's Driver
Who Became Archbishop

Dunstan Bukenya and James Kaye

The most inspiring person in our Church of Uganda is none other than His Grace the Archbishop of the Church of Uganda, the Most Reverend Livingstone Mpalanyi Nkoyoyo. It was most unexpected that this bishop should become archbishop because of his very humble academic background, but the story of how he became the archbishop can be a great lesson to both Christians and non-Christians in the world. Nkoyoyo's election gives us a very good example of God's choice, which sometimes may defy all the standards of academic achievement, experience, and others, set by humans.

Archbishop Nkoyoyo was born on 4 October 1938 in a village called Busimbi in Mityana District in Buganda region. He was the son of Erisa Wamala Nkoyoyo, who was then a traditional Ssaza Chief in the Kabaka's (King's) government. His mother was Naume Nakintu Nkoyoyo. The young Nkoyoyo went to school at Lubiri Primary School, and then Mityana Secondary School. Due to uncertainties in life, the youthful Nkoyoyo left secondary education and moved on to study motor mechanics. Although being a motor mechanic is no disgrace, at this time in the history of Uganda it was only considered suitable for those who failed to continue in the mainstream of education.

After his training, Nkoyoyo started his career as a mechanic in the Uganda Company and that is where he came to realise the salvation of Jesus Christ. He recalls the day when he was saved. That was 18 March 1959. Being saved proved to be a turning point in the life of the young man. Shortly after, he began to preach casually and became active in church activities. When he left the Uganda Company, he told his friends that he had decided to become 'God's mechanic'. Directly quoting his own words during his interview with *Involvement* magazine (September 1995 issue), he said, 'From there, I went on to be a mechanic of God's people. Right now, I am in Jesus' garage.'

Soon, he made contact with Bishop Lutaaya, who was then the Bishop of the Diocese of West Buganda, and he became the Bishop's driver and mechanic.

Before undertaking any further training, he served as a casual preacher at Nakibanga Church and Kiweesa Church – both in Mityana Diocese. He then trained for Lay Readership in Kisugu Church of Uganda, which was then in Namirembe, the Mother Diocese. He remained there until 1964.

He got married to Ruth Nkoyoyo in 1965, and the couple have two daughters and three sons.

From 1967 to 1969 Nkoyoyo studied for ordination at Buwalasi College and Bishop Tucker Theological College in Mukono. On Uganda Martyrs' Day, 3 June 1969, he was ordained deacon at Namugongo Martyrs' Shrine, and after six months, in January 1970, he was priested. After his ordination, he served in Kasubi Church as priest until 1974. After Kasubi, he was transferred to Nsangi Church where he served as priest until 1976. The Christians of Kasubi and Nsangi still say that they feel the effects of what was done by Mpalanyi Nkoyoyo. They describe him as having been an energetic and hardworking clergyman. Some of his many projects include the building of churches and houses for pastors.

His boundless energy and planning ability were quickly recognised. When the church needed a co-ordinator for the massive centenary celebrations marking 100 years of the Christian faith in Uganda, Nkoyoyo was assigned that great task. He was also appointed as Archdeacon of Namirembe from 28 December 1976. Nkoyoyo did such good work as centenary celebrations co-ordinator that he became even more popular.

From that time on, Nkoyoyo was a well-known figure. The church began to send him on tours and courses outside the country to improve his natural ability. In December 1978 he went to Ghana in West Africa. From there he went to the United Kingdom to gain experience in European churches. Here he remained until 1980. It was while he was in Britain that he was informed of his appointment as Assistant Bishop of Namirembe in 1980. Back in Uganda, he was consecrated in St Paul's Cathedral, Namirembe, on St Andrew's Day, 30 November 1980. In 1982, he was sent back to Britain, this time for developmental studies.

He was made a diocesan bishop in 1984 and moved to the newly established Diocese of Mukono. Nkoyoyo worked very successfully to put his new diocese on the map. In his new diocese, he was respected as a spiritual and moral pastor, a talented preacher, and a person interested in developmental issues.

In Mukonyo Diocese, Nkoyoyo made the Department of Mission very strong. He appointed a mission co-ordinator, and steps were taken to spread the Gospel to the more remote parts of the diocese, including the islands of Lake Victoria. Now, the mission has a motorboat to tour the islands, and there is a pastor in charge of this work.

In the material development of the diocese, many undertakings were established, including orphanages, a home for the aged, educational institutions, a health centre, a diocesan farm, a conference centre, and an improved system of transport.

What surprised many people was that Bishop Nkoyoyo was an uneducated mechanic, but God enabled him to work more cleverly than some highly educated people. By the time he was elected Archbishop, his Diocese of Mukono ranked as number one in both spiritual and material welfare among the dioceses of the Province of the Church of Uganda.

After ten years of his service as Bishop of Mukono Diocese, on 6 December 1994, Nkoyoyo was elected by the House of Bishops of the Province of the Church of Uganda as the sixth Archbishop of the Church of Uganda. He was the first ever Muganda to become an archbishop and, although many

archbishops have been elected from the West, North and
East of Uganda, Nkoyoyo was the first to be elected from the
Central region.

For many years, following Archbishop Leslie Brown, the
election of an archbishop was greatly influenced by the political
leadership. In Nkoyoyo's case, it was because of his ability.
He was more welcome than any of his predecessors and he
was seen as the man who could unite the different ethnic
groups in the Church of Uganda.

The interesting thing about Nkoyoyo's election as Archbishop was, firstly, that he was a man of very little education
compared with many bishops in the Church of Uganda who
are well educated, indeed, giants in the academic world. Some
are holders of MA and PhD degrees. Also, the Provincial
Assembly had already passed a resolution that no one without
at least a bachelor's degree was eligible for election as bishop,
and therefore no Archbishop could be without a degree.
When it came to the election of Nkoyoyo, the bishops overlooked this resolution since he was already a diocesan bishop.
He was consecrated and enthroned as Archbishop of the
Church of Uganda on 29 January 1995.

In spite of his lack of education, Nkoyoyo was welcomed
by all, including the foreign missionaries in the country. Tudor
Griffiths of the Church Missionary Society, then a tutor at
Bishop Tucker Theological College, described Nkoyoyo as 'a
man with natural intelligence and ability'. Another well-wisher
and supporter of the Church of Uganda, based in Britain
and formerly a tutor at Bishop Tucker College, Dr Kevin
Ward, in his editorial note to the November 1995 issue of
the *Newsletter of the Church of Uganda*, wrote:

The election as Archbishop of Uganda of Livingstone
Mpalanyi Nkoyoyo has been widely welcomed in all parts
of the Church of Uganda.

The least reason for rejoicing is that, after the election
of archbishops from the other parts of Uganda, it was

time for the Central Region to have its turn. Much more significant is the general perception of Bishop Nkoyoyo as a man of great integrity, faith and honesty. It was recognised that he had done a really good job as Bishop of Mukono, both as a pastor and in the material development of the diocese. There is a wide expectation that some of the difficulties which the church has faced in recent years in its spiritual life will be addressed in a profoundly serious way under Archbishop Livingstone's leadership.

Nkoyoyo has been described by his wife Ruth as a man who loves children, a good husband, a careful planner and a generous pastor. Indeed, this man has won the admiration of our political leaders and of the six million members of the Church of Uganda. He is known as a friend of other churches and other religions in Uganda. He is a uniting force, and his enthusiasm for development is always in evidence.

No wonder that His Grace the Archbishop of the Church of Uganda, one-time mechanic and driver, has become the cornerstone for the development of our church. He is, indeed, an inspiring Man of God.

Prayer for Africa

Prayer in Swahili, a language originating in the coastal area of East Africa, influenced by Arabic and the local African languages, and spoken in Uganda, Tanzania and Kenya.

Namshukuru Mungu, Baba yetu wa Mbinguni kwa kupata nafasi hii ya kuombea mambo mbalimbali katika Bara la Africa: Naombea Kanisa katika Bara la Africa, litie Kanisa nguvu liweze kuendelea na kukua katika upendo no kuzidi kukujua na kutimiza mapenzi yako. Wabariki Maaskofu, Wachungaji na wote wafanyao kazi yako;

Naombea familia zote, pamoja na ndoa za Kikristo. Uziimarishe na kuziangalia ili kila mtu aishi maisha matakatifu na ya kukupendeza wewe;

Naombea Chama cha Mama katika Bara la Africa. Naomba Mungu uwatie akina mama wote nguvu wapate kukujua kwa moyo wao wote;

Nawaombea wajane, yatima na wale wote ambao hawana msaada kutoka mahali popote. Nakusihi ukawape msaada toka kwako ee Mungu;

Naombea kazi ya Maendeleo katika Kanisa lako Mungu. Nawaombea wote walio na huduma ya ujenzi wa Mahospitali, Makanisa, Shule za Msingi na Sekondari watie nguvu katika huduma yote waifanyao kwa jamii yako;

Nawaombea wasafiri wanaokwenda kufanya kazi yako, mahali popote Ulimwenguni. Walinde na kuwatia nguvu katika huduma yako;

Nawaombea vijana katika kanisa pamoja na wale ambao hawakujui wewe Yesu Kristo. Naomba uwafungue macho ya Kiroho wapate kukujua wewe uliye Mtakatifu.

The same prayer, in English:

Almighty God our Heavenly Father, thank you for this time
you have given us to pray for Africa.

We pray for the Church of Christ in Africa, for its growth,
whole people of God and its leaders, especially Bishops, Pastors
and Evangelists that they may carry on to proclaim the Good
News of Jesus Christ and to bring wholeness and life to
human beings.

We pray for families and marriages that they may grow in
faith and love one another.

We pray for Mothers' Union activities as they continue to
witness to your truth. Strengthen their faith as they carry on
this ministry.

We pray for the poor, the oppressed, for the unemployed,
the destitute, for the widowed and for orphans, for the sick
and suffering and for all those in any need.

We pray for development activities, education, health, agricul-
ture and all other activities to improve the economy.

We pray for those whom you have called to send out, to
preach the Gospel. God; inspire them by your Holy Spirit.

We pray for the youth, and those who have not known you.
Lord, guide your servants as they minister to them. Amen.

Reflection

Mpalanyi Noyoyo has enormous energy and works incredibly
hard for God and for the people. He is both practical and
spiritual. His life of outgoing love stems from his conversion
to Christianity and his continuing openness to God's own love.

Discussion and Action

1. Many people have been surprised that Mpalanyi Noyoyo
   has achieved so much, because he is not highly educated.
   Does the world, including our own country, place too much

Children in Uganda
Simon Curl

value on formal education at the expense of spirituality
and love and commitment to the people.

2. What may we do to enable more of God's people to be
   doers and givers towards a better world?

People of Kenya

Godfrey Ngungire Wanjohi is a link person between his own Kikuyu people and the Masai people. He lives with his family in Kagongo near Othaya, on the edge of the Aberdare Mountains. He is an inspector of schools. He also works in development for the Church and regularly goes to the Masai town of Dol Dol, a drive of 160 kilometres, which takes at least three hours because the last 60 kilometres of the road are unsurfaced dust and gulleys. The journey, which links the Masai and the Kikuyu people, is from richly productive volcanic soils, where good farming is the norm, into the arid lands of Mukogodo, where only cacti and thorn bushes thrive, and goats and cattle scratch a living from the dust-laden clumps of grass.

When Godfrey arrives in the Mukogodo region he goes to many small communities, where he talks to the people about the issues and problems facing them, and buys honey. The honey is an excellent means of uniting the people. The cacti of the dry lands provide a superb environment for the bees. The Masai people make the wooden hives and hang them up in the trees. Isaac Keshine is a young Masai who lives in Dol Dol, where he refines and bottles the honey before it is taken to be sold in the churches in Godfrey's home area. The wax is also taken to be made into candles which are sold or used in the churches. The money earned is used by the Masai to supplement their diet and to send the children to school.

Cyrus Muturi Mwanike was born in the early 1950s on the slopes of the Aberdare Mountains in Kenya. As a young boy, he looked after his grandfather's goats and then went to school. While working for the Swedish Pentecostal Mission in Kenya he became a Christian. He is now a teacher and has taught in many schools in Nyeri District, Central Province. He is married with six children, and, besides his teaching, is heavily involved with planning and organising many church and youth activities with the Kenya Anglican Youth Organisation. He has been to England twice as a result of the link between KAYO and Christians Aware. Cyrus's memories of his grandfather (which follow) are a vivid reminder that relations between the Kikuyu and Masai people have not always been friendly.

My Grandfather

According to the information in my grandfather's identity card, he was born in 1877 in Nyeri District of Central Province in Kenya. He was initiated into manhood in 1897, was married to one wife, and they had four children, two boys and two girls.

As a young man, my grandfather was a warrior and went out with others to fight the Masai people, with whom the Kikuyu were constantly at war. As he advanced in age, he settled and became a tiller of the land, growing arrow-root and herding sheep, cattle and goats. These were the main sources of his wealth.

He was also a honey-gatherer, and used to be in the Aberdare Forest for weeks with others of his group, and they would come home with leather bags full of sweet, fresh honey which was used to make ceremonial beer. He would also spend a lot of time making beehives, taking them to the forest and then treating them with sweet-smelling herbs to attract the bees quickly.

I used to help my grandfather quite a lot. Every day I would go with him to look after his flocks of sheep, goats, and sometimes the cows. He had a lot of these, and so was regarded as a wealthy man, which, in fact, he was, according to the standards of wealth in his time.

When the time came for me to go to school, he was

very unhappy because, to him, education was nothing but a waste of time. My father had at that time just come from a detention camp, only to find my elder brother and me both past school-going age and tied to animal-herding. My father insisted that we should go to school.

My grandfather died in 1970 at the age of 93, and at the time of his death I was in Form Three. His memories are alive in me.

Building Together

In this poem about the building of a church in Kenya, Cyrus communicates the spirit of a KAYO and Christians Aware work camp.

Come, come, come,
it's time to choose the site.
Choose it, choose it and don't hesitate
for your choice may be the best.

Come, come, come, we've finished digging!
It's time to lay the foundation.
For here must be the steel and concrete.
The house of the Lord must be firm.

Come, come, come, we've laid the foundations!
Now it's time to lay the bricks.
The voluminous ones first,
and they must be 'nine by nine'.

Come, come, come, the walls are up!
Now it's time to put on the roof.
A strong roof it must be,
to stand the trials of the strong winds.

I have timber; you have nails;
he has tiles; they are artisans.
The house is ready. You can see it.
Let's all go in and worship the Lord!

Allan Mwangi Wanjohi was born in the early 1950s in Othaya
Urban Council area in Nyeri. After his schooling, he went
to Kenyatta College for teacher training and then enrolled
with United States International University where he studied
Guidance and Counselling. Now, he is a teacher at Munyange
Secondary School where he specialises in Guidance and
Counselling. Besides working at the school, he is also anxious
to see development in the local community.

Iriaini Cattle Dip

I am chairman of the cattle-dip project in my local village.
This project is in progress and all we do is organise the
local people who gather two days a week, for two hours,
to help build it.

The Church of the Province of Kenya (CPK) youth at
Iriaini Church help in a lot of things, including building
the cattle dip. Since the church here is a very new timber
building we also still have a lot of work there. I, and other
members of the church, are involved in many projects
and they all require money, so progress is quite slow.

A Laboratory for Munyange Secondary School

My school is entirely supported by the local community
except for the pay of the teaching staff. This is done by
the government. Hence it is far from easy to have all the
educational aids that we need. I thought of mobilising the
local community to help build a school laboratory, since
we didn't have one. The parents managed to give some

A Work Camp in Progress
Jane Walton-Loxton

money, but the manual labour – which did not require much skill – was provided by the local youth. They reported tirelessly to the building site every day and managed to finish the building.

The four walls are now complete. However, equipping the laboratory with necessary apparatus is another matter. Because of the general poverty of the community, it will take a longer time to obtain the apparatus. I am trying my best to organise for a donation to equip it. The local youth is always ready to help with manual work when they are called to supply this.

James Muriuki trained as a primary school teacher and taught for six and a half years before God called him to train as a full-time church worker. He was ordained priest in the Anglican Church in 1992. I visited James' childhood home, a farm high up on the slopes of Mount Kenya where his mother, our hostess, lives and works. The farm buildings and home are perched on the hillside, huddled together and including a shop and a very large sitting room, where people from the surrounding community, mostly members of the same clan, gather on most evenings. Sometimes suppers of the farm produce, including potatoes, avocado pears, arrow-root and paw-paw, are shared. The community is gradually building the local church. James built his own house just before he married his wife Jane. It is slightly apart from the other buildings, mainly of wood and with stone foundations. The farm is of twelve acres, which is large for a family farm. Its main work is in tea, cattle, pigs, maize and tomatoes.

James has spoken a lot about the differences he has seen in the two professions of teaching and ministry in the Church. He used to think that 'church ministry' would be easy and without hardships, but has now learnt that in any way of life there are ups and downs.

He writes: The ministry of the Church has been a great

encouragement, and has exposed me to very many opportunities which I otherwise would not have had. It has given me the opportunity to see new lands and people of different cultural backgrounds and different ways of understanding life. It has opened my eyes. I am looking forward to more experiences, and to sharing with people of other nations and other cultural backgrounds.

James is interested in:

Traditional Marriage Customs

Long ago in Kenya, marriage was not a private, but a community affair. Even up to now, marriage, whether taking place in church, or according to custom, it is not something private. All parties concerned must be involved.

Apart from the bride and groom, who must have taken time to get to know one another, to love one another and to spend time of courtship together, I want to say that the parents of both must be informed. They will give the go-ahead. The parents will come together for negotiations. The parents of the groom will visit those of the bride. They will carry presents in the form of money, animals or foodstuffs.

Some parents who have daughters will either impose conditions, or give them the go-ahead, after which all brothers and sisters of both the bride and groom will be informed. In short, the whole of the extended family is informed of the marriage that is about to take place. The people concerned will then publicise the matter to all friends and people known to them. The parents will extend an invitation to their friends; and those friends to their friends, and so on. So, on the wedding day, the people attending will include some who are not even known to the bride and groom, but they are all friends of friends.

It happens that, in some cases, the family of the bride will gather before the wedding day and draw up a programme of how they will escort their daughter on the day. They may also buy items for the couple such as a bed, mattress and all the bedding. They may supply other things, including money.

The parents of the groom likewise gather to prepare for the incoming important visitor. They too will draw up a programme of how to meet and welcome their son and his wife into the family. They may decide to buy this couple a cow, which will then be presented to them on the date of the wedding. They will organise the reception which will take place after the wedding. They may give voluntarily the foodstuffs to be prepared on the day.

In all these activities, the people of the groom's family will organise who will do what, and when. All services will be given freely. Nobody expects to be paid.

Weddings are normally held on Saturday, between 10 am and 2 pm and thereafter the reception follows. The reception goes on until the following day, Sunday, although many people are trying to discourage this because of the expenses involved. Some of us are trying to encourage people to have simple church weddings. These are much less expensive.

This photograph of a simple Masai wedding shows the
bride and groom wearing traditional Masai costume,
which they would already have. The groom is signing the
register, watched by the bride and the Anglican priest,
Joseph Ranja Ole Mepukori.

Joseph Ranja Ole Mepukori was a policeman before be became an Anglican priest. He is a Masai, married to Esther, and they have five children. They live in their own homestead, which is surrounded by fierce thorn fencing, and includes their home, and land and shelter for the cattle and goats. His parish is in the Masai area of Kenya, in the semi-arid area to the north-west of Nanyuki. He works with two evangelists and with the teachers in the nursery school and the polytechnic college. There are many problems including the lack of resources for the schools, the poor health of many of the people, and above all the lack of water. In 1991 and 1992 a terrible drought hit the whole area, and many people and cattle died. Joseph and the evangelists have a huge area to cover and they mostly walk in search of the people, who are nomadic and therefore move about all the time. Joseph's normal day begins at around 7 am when he sets off to find the people, asking the first group he comes across where others may be found. He is perhaps a twenty-first-century equivalent of the early Celtic Christian wanderers who were not always sure which direction they would go in or where they would pause or stay for the night. He sometimes sleeps in the manyattas, returning home the next day, or the day after that. He carries his own bright ochre-coloured blankets and also his food, because most of the people are so poor, keeping alive on the traditional milk and blood. Less than 20 per cent of the people have a settled home where they may grow a few food crops.

The Masai people are not easily attracted to Christianity and Joseph and the evangelists work with everyone whether they are Christian or not. One way of building understanding is to bring some of the Masai traditions and prayers into the churches, which is a mark of respect for the Christian Masai and also for the traditionalists. Traditional music and dancing are included in Christian worship and the stories and prayers of the people are used.

This is a traditional Masai prayer, now used in Christian worship:

Almighty and powerful God,
God of the Ancestors,
the black God who is the God of peace,
I come out having nothing,
being naked,
waiting for you, O God, to clothe me.
I am blessed, and you are the one who has blessed me.
You satisfy me with blessed gifts that come from you,
as you promised.
I will wait the fulfilment from you, O God,
because you said so.

Rahab Wanjiru lives with her parents on ten acres of land where they grow maize and keep cattle. Rahab has built a small rural tannery on the farm. She buys cattle skins and tans them into leather. She hopes to learn how to make bags and shoes. She is also keen to share her skills and to train others, especially some of the Masai people.

David Kariuki is a tailor who lives at Wiyumiririe. He began work with one sewing machine and now has three, and a shop where he takes orders for school uniforms and other clothes. He also has a small farm with cattle, sheep and vegetables, and he acts as the subpostmaster for his community. He delivers the letters to the people's homes.

Lucy Nancy Karya was born in Othaya, Nyeri, at a place known as Ngaru, in a family of seven girls and one boy. She trained in dressmaking at Nyahururu Craft Training Centre for one and a half years and she is an enthusiastic Christian. She has written about her local church:

Our local church is called Ngaru. It is in a large parish in the diocese of Mt Kenya West. We started to build our church in 1989 but up to now we have not yet managed to finish it. God will help us to get the money to complete it.

Our church has many different groups: Sunday school, Brigade, Youth (Kenya Anglican Youth Organisation) and Mothers' Union. I am one of the KAYO group. I am choir-mistress and I enjoy this job very much. We help elderly people, and we have done many things in our church. We have officials in our KAYO, and they are all very active in doing the work of God. I love them so much.

Charles Mwangi Welu is the secretary for Githi Parish. He also runs the youth programme and teaches in the Sunday school. He is a primary school teacher and games assistant. He runs clubs for farming, rabbits and care of wildlife. On his own farm he grows bananas and coffee, and he keeps pigs, goats, cows and hens. He is the secretary for his extended family, which means that he arranges meetings and social occasions and writes up the notes. The family meetings are called when there is the need to raise school fees or to help a relative who is ill. There may be a need to help family members with transport, especially during the rainy season. Sometimes help is given in campaigns for piped water or electricity, or for small pieces of land.

Stanley Murimi is 59 years old. He trained in building construction and worked for 20 years as a building foreman. After that, he changed to self-employment and has been selling building materials for the past 16 years. While self-employed, he also farmed in a small way, growing coffee, tea, and keeping a few dairy cattle. He has spoken about the co-operatives in his home area:

261

In my area, people have smallholdings from half an acre to about ten acres. In one division, they form one co-operative society, for example, a Dairy Society, where they employ clerks, establish milk-collecting stations, with a pickup, a cooler, offices, etc. In one morning, they collect all the milk from members and take it to Kenya Creameries' Co-operative. They later sell all milk, or milk products after processing. The money thus gained is sent back to the Dairy Society so that it can pay all its members.

Coffee growers, tea growers, pyrethrum and sugar-plantation farmers, etc., each have a product co-operative which collects all the produce, sells it and later pays the farming members their rightful payment.

In some areas, a district may combine a number of co-operative societies of different products and form a Union of Societies. The union helps to buy or import/export as a unit, and later pays back to societies so that each can pay its members. That system works efficiently and economically because they can employ experts in any one field when necessary.

Dedan Waithoinji Mujiri went to school at the age of 10 and he was the youngest in his class. No parent would send a son to school earlier because it was considered that he was too young to learn. Girls customarily were not educated at all. Dedan's secondary education was disrupted by the Freedom War in the country in 1953. In 1954, he joined the School of Pharmacy in Nairobi and completed his course in 1957. Since then he has been employed as a pharmacist in various hospitals and is now providing pharmaceutical services to all health centres in his home area of Nyeri. He spoke about his role in developing a water tank for the people of his area:

The Kihone water project involved all the people in the area. It involved pumping the water from a small river in the valley to the highest point in the area where we built a tank so that the water could flow to any point in our villages.

We formed a committee. The chairman was the local sub-chief, and every person in the village who had a talent or expertise in any area was involved.

The water project was to cover a distance of four miles downhill. As I was responsible for supplying all the pharmaceutical products to our county council, I was in a good position to influence the council to take part in the project. I was able to secure four miles of metal water pipes from UNICEF through the port of Mombasa for Kihone.

We invited a local politician to a fundraising meeting. He bought us a water-pump engine. The water problems were solved until a bigger project was introduced in later years. This then absorbed our smaller project.

Gold

This poem by James Muriuki is dedicated to the community of Nairobi where there is crime and injustice. We are praying that this will stop, and that people will join the church and pray for others so that we can all be as one.

This poem is called 'Gold'. Gold represents the life of the small children who wander about the streets with nothing to do and nobody to look after them in this dangerous city.

Here a small boy
knowing not what to do,
moves about the streets of doom,
another GOLD is lost.
Mourning never seems to end.
Pray with me, my dear friend.
Stop all the misery
or another GOLD will be lost.
May the love of God touch all astray,

may the peace be with all who are lost
for peace in them will give them GOLD.
OUR CHURCH.

Reflection

A Masai story tells of three bulls, of three different colours, red, black and white. The bulls were great friends and went everywhere together. There was also a lion who often tried to kill one of the bulls, but he always failed because they were always together. At last the lion asked a hare to divide the bulls.

The hare agreed and first spoke to the white bull and the black bull telling them that the red bull was dangerous because of its colour. He told them to chase the red bull away, which they did. When the red bull was alone he was caught and killed by the lion, who then ate him.

Later, the same hare told the black bull that the white bull was dangerous because he could be seen in the distance by enemies. He told the black bull to chase the white bull away, which he did. When the white bull was alone he was caught and killed by the lion, who then ate him.

Finally the lion went to the black bull and told him that he had eaten his two brothers, and now he would eat him, because there was no one left to defend him. The black bull realised his foolishness, but it was too late. The lion killed him and ate him.

Discussion and Action

The Kenyan people, like most African people, are members of their communities before they are individuals. Their value as individuals comes from their membership of the community. Look at the various ways in which the people you have met in this section work for their communities.

What can we give to our local communities?

Discuss the implications of the Masai story for the people in any community, anywhere in the world.

ROOTS AND WINGS

Dove of Peace and Justice
Jane Walton-Loxton

Young Horizons

The earth and the heavens
come together, touch, merge.
Familiar forms, firm, solid
and deep-rooted,
are enfolded and taken up
into the light,
the intangible and
moving, changing sky.

So the long unchanging,
the rootedness of all our human life
may trust strange wings
and rise to heights unknown,
to new and wondrous energy,
to courage and to hope,
for richer life and
paths towards the sky